iPad and iPhone
VIDEO

Film, Edit, and Share the Apple Way

JEFF CARLSON

PEACHPIT PRESS

iPad and iPhone Video:
Film, Edit, and Share the Apple Way

Jeff Carlson

Peachpit Press

www.peachpit.com

To report errors, please send a note to errata@peachpit.com
Peachpit Press is a division of Pearson Education

Senior Editor: Susan Rimerman
Production Editor: David Van Ness
Copyeditor/Proofreader: Scout Festa
Indexer: Karin Arrigoni
Composition: Jeff Carlson
Cover Design: Aren Straiger
Interior Design: Mimi Heft

ISBN 13: 978-0-133-85476-3

ISBN 10: 0-133-85476-0

10 9 8 7 6 5 4 3 2 1
Printed and bound in the United States of America

For family, near and far

Acknowledgments

If you're an aficionado of Acknowledgments pages (and if you're reading this, you probably are), you know that no book happens without the help of a lot of people. Sure, I do the word-writing. And I'm something of an anomaly in that I also do all the layout, screenshots, photos, and other artwork. Sounds like a one-man show, yes?

Oh heavens no. You'd be reading far too many occurrences of "that" and instances when I typed "dialog" instead of "dialogue" without the precise and speedy work of my copyeditor, Scout Festa.

If it weren't for editors Susan Rimerman and Karyn Johnson, this book wouldn't exist at all. Don't forget the rest of the team at Peachpit Press, including Nancy Davis and Nancy Aldrich-Ruenzel, who keep the whole operation running.

Although I do the layout, David Van Ness ensures that I didn't screw anything up and, more important, shepherds the InDesign files to the printer and ebook production teams. (And this time around he did it on a tight schedule, although perhaps in book publishing it's always a tight schedule.)

Speaking of layout, Mimi Heft designed a wonderful InDesign template that is, honestly, a joy to work in. Trust me, I've had to work with templates that are a nightmare—it makes a huge difference.

Before you go further, flip to the end of the book and look over the index created by Karin Arrigoni. Indexers are typically unheralded, but in a book like this, a top-notch index is invaluable. (A search feature is just not the same as an index.)

Closer to home, I owe a huge debt (repaid in hard cider and chocolate, no doubt) to my friends and colleagues Jeff Tolbert and Agen G.N. Schmitz. Jeff, a master of technology and music, wrote the chapter on using GarageBand. Agen, a master of all things, tackled the chapter on sharing projects and videos.

I also want to thank my friend Mason Marsh for his ideas, his encouragement, and the loan of his GoPro.

And most of all, I must thank my wife, Kimberly, and my daughter, Eliana, not only for being impromptu models and for being exceptionally patient at times, but for providing fulfillment to my already fortunate life.

Contents

Introduction

In 2001, I was on vacation in Alaska with a brand-new compact Canon camcorder that recorded video to tiny MiniDV cassette tapes. I could fit the camera in one of the many big pockets of my cargo pants (which might say as much about the fashion of the time as about the state of technology). Although I always try my best to disconnect my work brain when I'm on vacation, I couldn't help noticing the other cameras that people were carrying: many compact point-and-shoot cameras, a few larger SLR (single-lens reflex) or digital SLR models, and a smattering of compact camcorders like mine.

And then I saw that one guy. He looked perfectly normal, a middle-aged man also on vacation, but balanced on his shoulder was a *Canon XL1S*. This camera was the top-of-the-line professional model, sporting three recording sensors (one for each color of light: red, green, and blue) to capture glorious standard-definition interlaced video, interchangeable lenses, and a $5000 price tag. Nothing about that guy looked like a professional photographer, so I imagined he was probably a doctor or lawyer or some other monied mucky-muck who would be in a position to tell an underling, "Get me the best camcorder for my vacation."

I'm sure you know where this is headed.

The video capability of the iPhone in my pocket absolutely blows away that man's camera. I know it's not a fair comparison, since more than a dozen years of technological advancement occurred between the two cameras. But I rarely see camcorders of any variety today. Granted, camcorders still have their uses—optical zoom if nothing else—but the reality is this: People no longer need to buy a separate video recorder when the camera on their phone or tablet performs as well or better.

And yet, the technology isn't the real story here. When you can record video anywhere using an iPhone, iPad, or iPod touch that's already at hand, you'll shoot more video and take more photos. Many of those will be snapshots and short clips, or maybe micro-compositions like those created in Vine and Instagram. But as you become more comfortable with shooting video, the more you'll want to take a more active role in shaping the movies that result. Do you want to share a hundred photos of your last vacation, or cut together a three-minute highlight video? (Answer: Probably both.)

And here's the kicker: You can do it all on the same device you use to capture the footage—not just hacking together a clip or two, but making a professional-looking high-definition movie with features that were, just a few years ago, available only on desktop computers.

This Book Is for You

Some books are written like manuals (remember those?), detailing everything a product can do: *Here's the information, in some structured order; do what you want with it.* That approach assumes anyone can pick up the book, regardless of experience or skill level.

I prefer to think *you're* reading this book—yes, *you*, a real person who's interested in learning about shooting and editing video on an iPad, iPhone, or iPod touch. To do that, I've needed to make some assumptions about you, which I've used to shape the focus and content of this book:

• First of all, you're smart, you're intellectually curious, and you have good taste (for choosing my book; I'm not above flattery!).

• You already know the basics of using an iPad, iPhone, or iPod touch—using gestures such as taps and swipes, syncing with a computer, connecting to the Internet, charging the battery, and otherwise taking care of your device. (Another book of mine, *The iPad Air & iPad mini Pocket Guide*, can get you up to speed on this front if you need.)

• You're new to recording video, or to working with video using iOS devices. Or, you're a casual shooter who wants to learn more—and there's plenty to learn.

• You want to learn how to capture better video using an iPhone, iPad, or iPod touch, and edit the footage using the same device. You can certainly take the video you shoot, import it into a Mac or Windows PC, and edit a movie using something like iMovie, Adobe Premiere Elements, or Final Cut Pro X. But that ability is beyond the scope of this book.

• You're not an advanced videographer. That means you're probably interested in considering a few add-ons (lenses, a tripod) for shooting video, but you don't have shelves of more advanced gear. This book covers a lot of information that pushes beyond the basics, but it doesn't go into advanced options. For that, I highly recommend buying the book *Hand Held Hollywood's Filmmaking with the iPad & iPhone*, by Taz Goldstein.

One thing I'm *not* assuming is the type of movie you have in mind. You may be documenting a vacation, grabbing quick video clips when inspiration strikes, conducting interviews, producing a podcast, or filming a short or feature-length movie. You don't have to be an expert to make a movie, so the advice in this book applies to all types of videos. There's no reason the next Oscar-winning short film can't be shot and edited on portable devices instead of traditional equipment.

Notes About This Book

As you read, you'll run into examples where I've adopted general terms or phrases to avoid getting distracted by details. For example, I may refer to the "computer" or the "desktop" as shorthand for any traditional computer that isn't an iPad or iPhone. Although an iOS device is most certainly a computer, I'm making the distinction between it and other computing devices, such as laptops, towers, all-in-one machines, and other hardware that runs OS X or Windows. When those details are important to a task, I note specific applications or computers.

The same general rule applies to iPad and iPhone models. For example, the iPad mini, despite its size, is still a fully functional iPad, so when I refer to "iPad" in general it applies to the iPad mini as well as to the larger, flagship model. Similarly, I don't always refer to specific models. Sometimes it's important, such as when I'm discussing the Slo-Mo feature of the iPhone 5s, the only model that offers it (as of publication time). Mostly, though, I'm talking about the models that run the latest version of iOS.

I also frequently refer to just the iPhone even though the information applies equally well to the iPod touch. I'm not being lazy, for two reasons: If I had to always type "iPhone, iPad, and iPod touch" I'd need to ask my publisher for more pages and it would test your patience and mine. Also, as I write this, the latest iPod touch Apple sells is the fifth-generation model, which was originally released in 2012. (In 2013 the company released an entry-level model with just 16 GB of storage and no camera.) I suspect that unless Apple has something up its sleeve, the iPod touch as we know it will soon disappear.

Don't be surprised when you frequently run across the phrase, as you just did, "As I write this." iOS devices and the software useful to photographers and videographers are advancing rapidly, which makes this an exciting topic to cover.

When directing you to specific areas within iOS, I use a shorthand for locating them. For example, to access the preferences for the Camera app, I'll point you to **Settings > Photos & Camera**. That translates to "open the Settings app and tap the Photos & Camera button" (1).

1 Photos & Camera settings

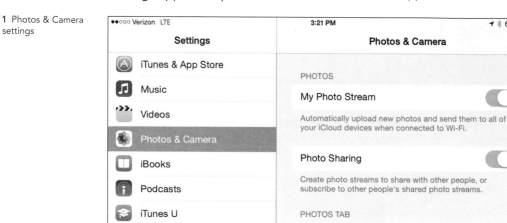

I mention many apps and products throughout the book, so instead of cluttering up the text with Web addresses, you'll find links in the "App and Equipment Reference" appendix.

To stay abreast of the changing field, be sure to visit my Web site, jeffcarlson.com, where I post updates and information related to books and projects.

Lastly, please sign up for my low-volume newsletter, where I keep readers updated on new projects and giveaways: http://eepurl.com/KYLFv.

Have fun recording and editing, and please feel free to contact me via my site or at jeff@necoffee.com with feedback!

iOS 8

Right before this book went to press, Apple announced iOS 8, the next major version of the operating system that runs the iPhone, iPad, and iPod touch. iOS 8 promises to bring several interesting changes to how the iPhone and iPad work with video.

For example, Apple will be rolling out iCloud Photo Library, a new way to store your photos and videos without the often confusing limitations of iOS 7's iCloud Photo Stream. The only limit to what can be stored in the cloud is how much you're willing to pay for storage; 5 GB is free, and paid plans begin at $0.99 a month.

The architecture of iOS 8 will become very important, too. Third-party developers will be able to offer extensions that make their products work within other apps. So, for instance, while you're working in iMovie you may be able to process a clip using Emulsio's tools for removing camera shake right in iMovie, without having to exit the app.

The Camera app also gains a new Time-lapse mode for creating time-lapse videos, something you need to turn to third-party apps to accomplish now (see Chapter 5).

iOS 8 isn't expected until fall 2014, so even though some information about the changes are public, I couldn't include them in this book (both because of the publishing schedule and because, as a registered iOS developer, I'm bound by non-disclosure agreements). When the time comes, I'll post updates to jeffcarlson.com detailing what's different from the information in this book.

CHAPTER 1

Video Crash Course

On most video productions, a lot happens before footage is recorded. Cameras are placed, shots are lined up, lighting is set, and subjects are positioned. The reality of shooting video with your iPad, iPhone, or iPod touch is probably the opposite: many spontaneous moments are captured because your device is easily at hand. What both situations share is a foundation of technical ability and purpose. Just because you're grabbing an unexpected event doesn't mean it has to be captured haphazardly.

Over years of watching movies, television, and online clips, we've all developed a visual language of photography in motion that separates careless shooting from purposeful capture. A steady frame, composition that features subjects with intent and balance, good audio, variety of shots (such as close-ups and establishing shots)—these characteristics separate footage that people want to see from video that's painful to watch. Once you have these foundations of video in your blood, even the most spontaneous captures you make will look better than careless ones. (And you'll also have a better sense of when to break those rules.)

Intent

I know this is a fuzzy concept to start off with, but let me encourage you to start with an idea of what the result of your video will be. Even if it's a nebulous idea, embarking on a video shoot helps you determine the best way to record it.

For example, let's say you want to preserve the look and feel of a day on vacation. You could make a mental checklist (or create a literal one if that helps) of landmarks and events scheduled for the day. Expanding beyond that, think about recording what surrounds a landmark. Is it crowded, serene, bright, dark, colorful? Is the landmark the only interesting item in the area to focus on? Perhaps the road to reach it was more of an adventure than the destination was. What does the area *sound* like? What aspects of the place do you want to convey to someone who isn't there?

With those questions in mind, we can break out a theoretical list of video clips to capture:

- Footage of the journey to reach the landmark.

- An *establishing shot* of the landmark and its immediate surroundings. (I'll talk more about shot types shortly.)

- Clips that focus on specific items in *close-up shots*, such as foliage or animals nearby, people who work or live near the landmark, or detailed elements of the landmark or event itself.

- Video of the area in general, often referred to as *B-roll footage*, that records the area's sound and gets a feel for the environment.

Now, before you start to feel overwhelmed with an abundance of planning, let's turn to something more spontaneous. A friend is doing something amusing that you want to capture on video. Even as you're pulling an iPhone from your pocket, you can be thinking of where to position your friend within the frame and where you should stand to capture the moment. Maybe she's telling a joke and you need to step back a bit to get her arm and hand gestures in the shot. Maybe she's about to jump on top of a table and belt out a song, in which case you want to include both the table and her in the frame.

The point is, with a small arsenal of video knowledge you can capture higher-quality footage, regardless of how planned or impromptu the situation is. Because here's the thing about photography, and especially video:

you often can't go back and get the shot. Your friend could re-enact the joke, but it might not be as good as the first telling. You may not return to the landmark on this trip. And so, whenever possible, you want to capture the best footage you can in the moment.

Video Format

Okay, let's jump back to more practical considerations, such as what format the iOS devices record in. Apple has made this part of the video process easy by limiting what its cameras capture. You don't need to worry about multiple file formats the way you do with camcorders and professional equipment.

All iPads since the iPad 2, iPhones since the iPhone 4, and iPod touch models starting with the fifth-generation capture high-definition (HD) video at either 720p (1280 by 720 pixels) or 1080p (1920 by 1080 pixels) (1.1). The "p" in the name stands for "progressive," which means every horizontal line for each frame is recorded; some non-Apple video devices record in 1080i, where "i" stands for "interlaced" and every other line in a frame is recorded.

▶ **NOTE** Although the camera captures every pixel for each frame, not every pixel is saved to memory. To prevent HD video from quickly overwhelming the storage on your device, the video is compressed. For example, pixels that remain the same between frames 1 and 2 are discarded in frame 2. However, the compression algorithms are good enough that you wouldn't know the difference.

1.1 Video sizes

720p

1080p

The cameras record video at 30 frames per second (fps), although some software can adjust that to 24 fps, the rate at which most theatrical movies are shot. The iPhone 5s is also capable of capturing 120 fps in its Slow-Mo mode. (When played back at regular 30 fps speed, the 120 fps footage appears in slow motion; I cover that in Chapter 2.)

▶ **NOTE** When I talk about cameras, I'm almost always referring to the rear camera, not the front-facing camera above the screen. The rear camera contains a better image sensor and optics; the front camera is designed for FaceTime video calls, which don't need the high resolution.

Composition

I'd argue that one of the biggest advantages to shooting video with an iPhone or iPad is the ability to view the scene using a larger screen, compared to a viewfinder or a camera's LCD screen. You can see clearly which objects appear in the frame and where they're positioned, and then adjust for better composition if needed.

You can find counterexamples to everything I mention here, so keep in mind that none of these suggestions are set in stone. But use them as a guide when framing your shots.

The Rule of Thirds

If every scene you record features a person in the middle of the frame, not only will all your shots become repetitive, but you'll also miss out on the possibilities of using the left and right areas to create more visually interesting compositions.

The "rule of thirds" imagines the frame split into three vertical and three horizontal areas (1.2). Some apps (though not Apple's Camera app) include the option to display a grid that helps you line up elements. Move the camera so the subject of your shot falls into one of the "thirds." If you're shooting a landscape, position the horizon line roughly a third of the distance from the top of the screen (to emphasize the ground) or a third from the bottom of the screen (to emphasize the sky) instead of bisecting the frame.

Mind the Background

The traditional reason for making note of what else is in the frame is to avoid tree branches that might look like they're growing out of someone's head. However, I think people are more forgiving about discerning faces from foliage, especially when shooting video. Instead, keep an eye out for other distractions, such as tourists wandering into the frame, signs or graffiti, or items such as litter that may escape someone's eye when they're on location but will draw the viewer's attention when viewed within the frame.

Sometimes, such distractions can be minimized in editing—for instance, you could cut to another view of a monument during the seconds that a tourist inadvertently walked across the front of the camera. More often the better solution is as simple as walking a few steps to reframe the shot.

Lead into the Frame

Taking the rule of thirds one step further, when someone or something is moving across the frame, give them room to move by showing the viewer where they're headed (1.3, on the next page). Use the "empty" two-thirds of the frame to help the viewer anticipate the direction or destination. (The flipside is to put someone at the edge of the frame facing out. Horror movies use techniques like this all the time to make viewers feel uneasy.)

Shot Variety

No matter what type of movie you're shooting, it's important to vary the composition of shots. Everything centered all the time is uninteresting. The type of shot can also affect the mood of the scene; an extreme close-up that includes a person's eyes and perspiring forehead evokes a different feeling than a wider shot where you see a person sitting at a desk. Here's a selection of shot types; the next time you're watching a movie or TV show, try to spot the shots and how often they're used.

- **Establishing shot.** This shot, usually framed wide enough to include many elements, is used to establish the geography or context of a scene (1.4). A few seconds of footage that includes the exterior of a mountaintop hotel tells the viewer where the next scenes occur (even if, as in most fictional shows, all of the interiors are shot on sound stages or at distant locations).

- **Medium shot.** Typically framed to include two or three people's torsos, medium shots, and variations thereof, are most common.

- **Close-up shot.** As its name suggests, the close-up shot involves positioning the camera so that most of the frame is filled by the subject (1.5). That can be a head-and-shoulders clip of someone being interviewed or a shot of a memorial plaque.

- **Cutaway/B-roll.** This type of footage can be a lifesaver during the editing process. It's anything in the surrounding area that is not the subject. When you're shooting, don't stop recording immediately when the action ends. Instead, linger on the scene, capture the sky, flowers, sculpture, hallways, desk clutter…anything that draws your eye and can be used later to better evoke the environment in which you were filming.

I want to emphasize that you don't need to plan a bunch of specific shot types for every project. What's important is that you're thinking of other variations while you're shooting so that you don't miss something that could be used later.

1.4 Establishing shot

1.5 Close-up shot

Audio

Have you ever attended a pre-release screening of a movie-in-progress? It makes you realize just how much polish is applied to a finished film. For example, nearly everything you hear has been re-recorded or processed. In one screening I viewed, the on-set audio was still present, and the actors' dialogue was much less distinct from the surrounding noise. Also, sounds such as footsteps, explosions, and even birds in the sky are all created and added later.

Audio is important, and professionals use many techniques to capture better audio than what's available from the camera's built-in microphone. But what about shooting with an iOS device? An iPhone has a decent microphone, but it's limited to objects that are fairly close to it. And the iPhone doesn't include a handy hotshoe on top on which to attach a microphone, as many video cameras and DSLRs do.

It is possible to record good audio with an iPhone or iPad—it just depends on what measures you're willing to take to do it. I think that's based largely on the type of video you're shooting: a travelogue of your vacation is much different than an interview with someone.

> ▶ **NOTE** I'm realistic enough to understand that you're not going to reach for a microphone at every opportunity. (Well, I'm not going to anyway.) I don't carry a mic with me everywhere, nor do I leave it connected to my iPhone. But for those times when you can be more deliberate about recording, the improved sound will be worth it.

Microphones

The first step is to record with something other than the iPhone's or iPad's built-in microphone. Three types of mics can help.

- If you're shooting a short distance from your subject, a shotgun or directional microphone captures audio from a narrow cone in front of the mic, minimizing the noise coming from the sides or from behind it.

- A handheld microphone such as the iRig Mic is great for doing interviews, recording a performance, or capturing other audio to which you can get close enough to position the microphone.

- For interviews in which your focus is on the audio of the person being interviewed, or if you're the one doing the talking and you want an unobtrusive microphone, buy a lavalier mic such as the Røde SmartLav. A lavalier clips onto a shirt, so it's hands-free and out of the way.

Some of the microphones, such as the iRig Mic, are designed to plug directly into the iOS device's headphone port (1.6). If you already own a microphone with an XLR-style plug, you can use an adapter such as the iRig Pre to bridge the gap between the mic and the iOS device. Also check out the online store KV Connection for inexpensive cable adapters.

1.6 iRig Mic

A Step Up: Røde VideoMic Pro

When you're ready for more audio options, consider Røde's VideoMic Pro, a shotgun microphone that sells for about $230 and doesn't rely on the iOS device for power (1.7). You'll want a mount such as the Padcaster or mCAMLITE to attach the mic, and an adapter to bridge the iPhone's or iPad's headphone connector and the microphone's 3.5mm plug.

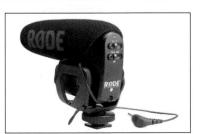

1.7 Røde VideoMic Pro

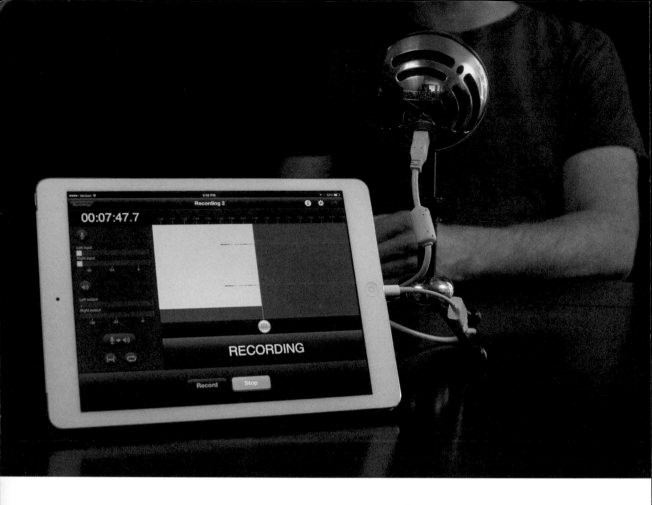

Another option, for iPad owners, is to use USB microphones, like those used for podcasting on your computer. With the addition of the Apple Lightning to USB Camera Adapter or the iPad Camera Connection Kit (for older models with 30-pin ports), you can plug a USB microphone into the iPad. (Some microphones require more power than the iPad is able to provide, so search the Web for your mic model before buying the adapter for this purpose.)

▶ **TIP** Don't forget about the earbuds that come with the iPhone. When you connect them to the headphone jack on the iPhone or iPad, the microphone included on the cable becomes the audio input for your movie. If you're looking to narrate what you're shooting as you film, this is a good way to do it. (Remember that you can add narration later while editing, which is a better idea to keep the scene's audio separate from the narration.)

External Recording

There's another way to tackle the audio issue, and that's to not worry about the audio the camera is recording. Instead, record audio separately to another iPhone, iPad, or iPod touch. This approach is practically required if you're shooting from a distance that's beyond what the camera can pick up.

For an interview, if you don't have a lavalier or handheld microphone, set an iPhone to record audio and place it just out of the frame, or put it in a shirt pocket. Even if you do have a microphone, connecting it to an external recording device avoids tangled cables and, more importantly, gives you a second copy of the audio.

If you're shooting something that involves more deliberate recording, like an interview or something scripted, it's helpful to use some sort of clapper or slate when you start. It doesn't have to be a real slate (the type you see in behind-the-scenes moviemaking footage), but something that introduces a sharp, loud sound that's easy to synchronize when you're editing.

▶ **TIP** Okay, this is seriously overkill for casual shooters, but if you want a great virtual slate, check out MovieSlate. Yes, you get the sound, but it also records timecode, shot information, sound information, and more. For our purposes, timecode—the movie industry standard for measuring recorded video and film—doesn't come into play when editing in iMovie on the iPad or iPhone. (But it is represented in Pinnacle Studio; see Chapter 3.)

Improve the Camera

In Seattle, the Fremont Solstice Parade is a photographer's dream. Fremont is a wildly eclectic neighborhood, so a parade that celebrates the changing of the season is full of color and character. Oh, and hundreds of naked bicyclists decorated in body paint.

One year my wife and I were finishing breakfast at a favorite diner when the procession of cyclists started streaming past the windows. I thought the parade was the following day, so I was without a camera—or was I? In the spirit of "the best camera is the one with you," I quickly grabbed my Palm Treo smartphone and started snapping photos.

Technically, I did capture pictures of the parade. Realistically, they were low resolution, poorly colored, and terrible.

If I were in the same position today using my iPhone 5s, the quality of the photos would be quite good. (I don't remember if I even bothered trying to shoot video with the Treo.) The technology in the current generations of iPhones and iPads is remarkable, both optically and in the image processing software that drives the lens.

Still, there are limitations. The camera is just one function out of many, and its size is severely restricted by the pocketable nature of the case design. There's no optical zoom—if you want something to be larger in the frame, you need to move closer (the digital zoom is decent in a pinch, but not nearly as good as optical). And you have no choice in the size or capability of the lens; it's designed to work well for all types of scenes, which means it doesn't excel in specific situations, like wide-angle views or close-up macro shots. Don't worry, though, because plenty of companies want to sell you add-ons that help overcome many of those limitations.

Shoot Steady

The number one way to set your video apart from most everything that's recorded with a smartphone or tablet? Steady, smooth motion. Yes, shaky footage has its uses, but steady motion is more polished and professional. Does that mean you need to haul a big tripod everywhere? Nope, alternatives abound. Here are a few of my favorites:

GorillaPod adjustable tripods

I own a few tripods, but often they're overkill for mounting an iPhone. Joby's GorillaPod models feature articulating legs that can be positioned on nearly any surface or wrapped around railings, tree branches, and other objects (1.8). If you're shooting handheld, extend the legs and use the GorillaPod as a handle. Some models offer a standard screw for connecting any camera, while others come with a bracket that fits over the iPhone.

The Glif

Studio Neat's Glif is a combination tripod mount (for attaching the iPhone to a tripod) and a stand that can hold the iPhone at an angle when you're editing or watching movies.

1.8 Glif mounted on a GorillaPod tripod

> ▶ **TIP** A quick search on Amazon or Google will reveal many methods of mounting an iOS device to a tripod. If you're looking for something light and portable that can be easily carried in a bag, Square Jellyfish makes Jelly Legs tripods, the Spring Tripod Mount, and the Micro Ball Head, which work well together. The company also makes versions that fit the iPad mini.

iStabilizer Dolly

A tripod is great for photographs, because it keeps the camera still. But video is motion, and sometimes moving the camera can be an effective way to tell a story (think of how many movies slowly push in on a character when they're seeing something unbelievable).

The iStabilizer Dolly is a small platform built on four wheels, with an articulating arm that holds the iPhone in place (**1.9 on the next page**). You can make smooth dolly moves (where the camera is doing the moving, versus zooming the lens) without introducing the jostle of walking. The platform can also be adjusted to make the wheels turn, enabling creative elliptical movements.

Mobislyder

Another option for smooth motion is the Mobislyder. It's a 12-inch track with a mount that slides horizontally or at an incline. And because it doesn't have wheels, like the iStabilizer Dolly, it's not subject to the smoothness of the surface it's rolling across.

Padcaster and Padcaster mini

You'll notice that the options thus far are made for the iPhone, since the device's size is much more amenable to shooting video (and the camera is still better than the iPad's). If you're shooting with an iPad, however, you're not limited to holding it in front of you like a dinner plate.

The Padcaster and the Padcaster mini are both fairly big steps up, but they're good steps. They feature tripod mounts for stability, but also include hotshoe mounts to add things like portable lights and microphones (1.10). The best part is the ability to add a high-quality lens in front of the iPad's camera.

mCAMLITE and Phocus Accent

Another step up, the mCAMLITE case for the iPhone is made of aluminum and includes a tripod mount, shoe mount, microphone, and a combination wide-angle/macro lens. The Phocus Accent is a similar, less expensive model with many lenses and other accessories available.

Lenses

As I mentioned earlier, the cameras in the iPhone and iPad are quite good, but limited in range. Several companies sell add-on lenses that fit in front of the camera to change your perspective.

Olloclip

For ease of use, the Olloclip is my choice for extra lenses. Its clever design includes two lenses that fit over the corner of an iPhone or iPad (1.11, **on the next page**). Don't want to use the wide-angle lens? Flip it around and use the fisheye. Or, unscrew one of those to reveal a macro lens. It doesn't require a special case (though Olloclip does sell one that offers a tripod mount) and doesn't take up much room. The company also offers a 2x telephoto lens with a polarizer and additional macro lenses for iPhone and iPad models.

iPro Lens System

The iPro Lens System offers better glass than the Olloclip (at a higher price) and requires a case to affix the lenses onto. For the iPad, the lenses attach to a clip that covers the iPad's camera. You can buy a wide-angle, super wide-angle, fisheye, macro, or 2x telephoto lens (or combinations).

PhotoProX

One challenge of the iPhone is that it doesn't cater well to bad weather or being underwater. The Optrix PhotoProX is a waterproof case that includes four interchangeable lenses. Although the first time you dunk your phone into water is nerve-racking, the case is well sealed (down to 33 feet). Even if you're not shooting an underwater documentary (or Bond film), the PhotoProX is nice to have in messy, muddy, or sandy conditions that threaten your iPhone.

Extra Power

Don't forget that shooting and editing video is demanding on your device's battery. If you expect to do a lot of recording, consider picking up an external power source such as a Mophie Juice Pack or external battery chargers.

▶ **TIP** Many companies offer external batteries, so let me save you some trouble. Visit the Web site The Wirecutter to learn what the editors there have (extensively) tested and recommend. That advice applies to all sorts of products, not just mobile accessories.

CHAPTER 2

Capture Video

You'd think shooting video would be basically the same as making still photos. Same hardware, same form factor, same act of pressing a button to capture and record photons. As we learned in the last chapter, though, video takes additional thought. I often feel like I need to swap in a video brain when I switch modes on my iPhone or iPad, because more factors of the scene demand my attention. I not only need to think about the composition of the scene, I need to imagine the composition as it might be in a few seconds or minutes after I tap the Record button.

I also need to think about what the finished product could look like. Even when I'm shooting something spontaneous, it's good to be aware of my surroundings so I can record B-roll footage that I can splice into the movie later. And I need to remember the audio, a dimension that doesn't apply to still photos but that can be vital for video. Am I getting enough ambient noise to impart a sense of where I am? Is my subject close enough to the microphone?

It all starts with the capture. You can't fake footage you never shot. Even if you go back to a location, all the variables—lighting, audio, people, weather—will be different. Become familiar with the ways iOS records video so you can concentrate on getting good content without being distracted by technical specifics.

Camera App

Apple's Camera app is intentionally bare-bones to make it easy for anyone to use. Some people might scoff at this and immediately look for a more powerful tool, which I'll get to shortly. But you can shoot good video using what's provided in the iPhone or iPad and never need advanced features.

To be honest, I end up using the Camera app most often, because of one key feature: I can access it from the lock screen without unlocking the device. That's the quickest way to start shooting, bypassing the need to locate and launch the Camera app.

When you press the Home button or the Sleep/Wake button to wake the device, touch the Camera button in the lower-right corner and swipe up. Or, from any app (including the lock screen), swipe up from the bottom of the screen to open Control Center and tap the Camera button (2.1).

2.1 Quick access to the Camera app

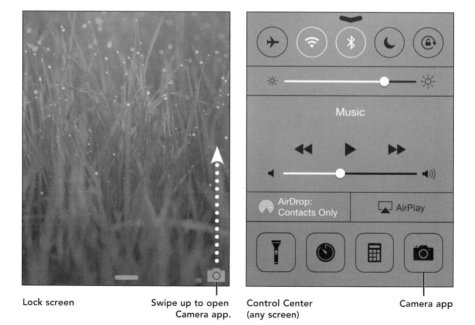

Lock screen   Swipe up to open   Control Center   Camera app
               Camera app.   (any screen)

▶ **TIP** Switch the device to Airplane mode if you're shooting for longer than a quick capture. You don't want a shot interrupted by an incoming call, text message, or notification. The easiest method is to bring up Control Center and tap the Airplane Mode button (top left in the figure above).

Choose Video Modes

Initially, the Camera app is set to Photo mode to capture stills. It's easy enough to switch to Video mode, although the control is surprisingly not obvious. The modes are listed on the side of the screen, but to switch among them, *swipe* up or down anywhere on the screen (2.2). On the iPad and the iPhone 5 and earlier, the modes include Photo, Video, and Square (a photo shot in a square aspect ratio); the iPhone 5s adds a Slo-Mo mode for slow-motion video capture.

▶ **NOTE** The iPhone receives the latest-generation features that Apple cooks up, mostly because more people capture photos and videos using the iPhone versus the iPad. But even among iPhone models you'll find different features. The iPhone 5s is the only model (as of this writing) that offers the Slo-Mo mode. The iPad and iPhone 4s and older don't offer the ability to capture a snapshot while shooting video. Also, the iPad lacks an LED flash.

2.2 Change camera modes.

Swipe vertically anywhere to change mode.   Modes

Use the Flash

The flash on the back of the iPhone 5s is remarkable for how it can balance tones in still images. When shooting video, however, enabling the flash causes the LED to remain on. Although that often results in a tabloid-style spotlight (and subjects squinting against the bright light), it'll work in a pinch if it's just too dark to record anything without it.

Tap the Flash button (with the lightning bolt) and choose Auto, On, or Off. I suggest switching it to Off instead of Auto to ensure that it doesn't fire unexpectedly.

Focus and Exposure

The Camera app does its best to pick the right focus and exposure for a photo or video, but it often needs a little help. It recognizes faces and displays a yellow box around them before you record, and generally looks to the middle of the screen for a focus point. You can (and should) specify items by tapping once on them; a square focus box appears (2.3).

2.3 Tap an area to set the focus and exposure.

Focus and exposure reference

When you tap the screen, the Camera app not only uses that point to establish focus but also determines the overall exposure for the scene.

As you record, the app attempts to adjust both focus and exposure to compensate for changes in the scene—as you move from a dark, shaded area to a sunlit one, for example, or even just clouds passing overhead and blocking direct sunlight. You can override that behavior by locking both values:

Touch and hold the area on which you wish to base the focus and exposure. After a second, the AE/AF LOCK (auto-exposure/auto-focus) indicator appears (2.4). While you record, neither attribute changes. The setting remains after you stop recording a clip, ready for the next clip.

2.4 Focus and exposure locked

Recording

Perhaps you noticed the not-so-subtle giant red button at the side of the screen. Tapping it begins recording, as you would expect, but what happens while frames are being saved to memory involves more than just pointing the camera in the right direction.

- The app will attempt to keep items in focus if AE/AF isn't locked.

- While recording, tap the screen to choose a new focus and exposure point. If you locked focus before shooting, the lock is removed (so don't accidentally brush the screen). You can touch-and-hold to choose and lock a new focus and exposure. Doing so takes a steady touch, though: a quick jab at the screen will create distracting camera shake.

- On the iPhone 5 and later, tap the additional shutter button that appears to capture a still photo without disturbing the video recording. The picture is saved at video resolution (1080 by 1920 pixels), not at the camera's full still-image resolution (2448 by 3264 pixels).

- Pinch outward with two fingers to zoom in while shooting. Remember, the zoom is digital, not optical, so the image quality drops when you enlarge it in the frame. It's also something you can do while editing, so my preference is to not zoom and capture the highest-quality version I can. I talk about reframing—cropping—clips in iMovie in Chapter 3.

- Tap the Record button again to stop recording.

▶ **TIP** In the previous chapter I shared a few options for steadying the camera and moving it smoothly, but another important consideration applies while you're filming. When the camera is in motion, try to move slowly and deliberately. When you whip the camera back and forth, your footage becomes a blur and the viewer can't easily track what's happening.

Portrait Orientation, or What Not to Do

I don't want to get between you and your creative vision, but let's settle this right here: Although you *can* capture video when holding the iPhone or iPad in its portrait (tall) orientation, *don't do it*. Please please please pretty please.

Nearly all video, and every outlet that presents video, is horizontal. If you shoot vertical, your clip appears in a narrow slice in the middle of the screen (**2.5**). Not only is it a waste of space, but it makes it difficult to see what you shot and minimizes any effect you were working toward. Please. Really. Don't.

2.5 Footage shot vertically is a waste of space. (Screenshot from an iPhone 5s.)

Review a Clip

When you finish a clip, a small thumbnail of it appears at the bottom corner of the screen; tap it to view your Camera Roll. (If you launched the Camera app from the lock screen, you'll see only the clips you've recorded in that session, not the entire contents of the Camera Roll.) To play back the clip, do any of the following:

- Tap the large Play button in the middle of the screen. Or, tap the smaller triangular Play button that appears at the bottom of the screen (iPhone) or at the upper-right corner (iPad) (2.6). The initial Play button disappears after you've played the clip, so you need to use the other Play button (which turns into a Pause button) to control playback.

- While the video is playing, the playhead advances along the filmstrip at the top to indicate the position within the clip. Drag the playhead anywhere in the clip to jump to that section.

- For finer-grained control over positioning the playhead, touch and hold it for a second—the filmstrip stretches out to display a "zoomed in" portion of the clip.

Playhead   Filmstrip   Initial Play button   Play button

2.6 Playback options on the iPad

Trim a Clip

When you're reviewing a clip, you can trim the beginning and end to remove extraneous frames (such as if you needed to refocus or you were waiting for the action to begin). Most of your editing will be done in a dedicated app such as iMovie or Pinnacle Studio, so in general I ignore this feature. Sometimes, though, you'll want to shoot a quick video and share it right away without taking a side trip to an editing app. To trim a clip, do the following:

1. Touch the far left or far right edge of the filmstrip and start dragging the handle; the filmstrip gains a yellow border (2.7).

2. Drag the handles to isolate the section of the clip you want to keep. Any frames outside the handles will be removed.

3. Tap the Trim button.

4. In the dialog that appears, choose either Trim Original or Save as New Clip. If you opt to trim the original clip, the frames you excise will be gone permanently. Unless you truly don't want that section later, I advise choosing Save as New Clip.

2.7 Trim a clip.

Portion of clip to keep

Review and Adjust a Slo-Mo Clip

The Camera app's Slo-Mo mode is made possible by shooting at 120 frames per second (at 720p instead of 1080p). When played back at the standard rate of 30 frames per second, the action you shot during one second takes four seconds to play out.

Apple added a neat feature to Slo-Mo clips when you're reviewing them. Instead of playing the entire clip in slow motion, the video starts at normal speed, transitions to slow to accentuate the effect, and then returns to normal speed at the end. Here's how to control which portion of the clip appears slowed down in the Photos app.

1. Tap a Slo-Mo clip to view it; videos shot in slow motion appear with a dotted circle icon (2.8).

2. Drag the slow-motion handles to identify the section that appears slowed down.

2.8 Identifying and viewing a Slo-Mo clip

Slo-Mo icon

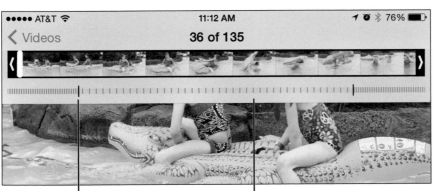

Slow-motion handle   Slow section

▶ **NOTE** The Slo-Mo section is retained when you share the clip (such as via iCloud Photo Stream), but not when the clip is imported into iMovie.

Delete a Clip

If the clip isn't worth saving at all, tap the trash can button at the lower-right corner to delete the clip.

Rolling with the Rolling Shutter

The iPhone, the iPad, and most other compact devices use what's called a "rolling shutter" to record video. When you begin shooting, the camera records light in horizontal bands starting at the top of the image sensor and moving down before going back to the top for another pass. Of course, the recording is happening so quickly it's as if each frame were being captured at once.

However, if you're shooting something moving faster than the shutter speed, you encounter the *rolling shutter effect*. Since the object is moving so quickly, it's changed position before the image sensor can grab a full frame, resulting in distortion.

Sometimes the distortion is wildly noticeable: recording a plane's propeller can make it seem like the aircraft is being kept in the air by floppy flower petals. But it can also creep into normal situations, such as panning the camera too quickly **(2.9)**. The solution is to move the camera steadily whenever possible, or try to avoid situations in which the rolling shutter effect might occur.

2.9 Those boats look like they're leaning in this whip pan, thanks to the rolling shutter effect.

FiLMiC Pro

Jumping from the Camera app to FiLMiC Pro is like eschewing a Mini Cooper in favor of a Porsche. The Porsche is a bit more difficult to drive, but it'll perform better and hew tighter to curves without slowing you down. FiLMiC Pro is designed for photographers who are more interested in controlling variables such as focus, exposure, and playback speed.

I'm not suggesting, however, that it's overkill for shooting family vacation videos. The beauty of the app is that you can use or ignore the advanced features, but you still get a better basic toolset to work with. (For example, FiLMiC Pro can capture video in slow motion, even if you don't own an iPhone 5s. If you do shoot with that model, you can choose among four slo-mo speeds.) I'll start with the fundamentals and then expand into many of the more interesting features.

Focus and Exposure

One of the best reasons to shoot using FiLMiC Pro is the ability to set focus and exposure independently using two separate reticules (2.10).

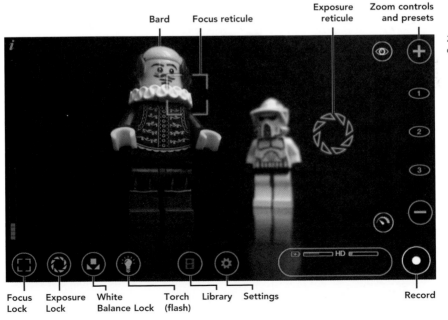

Bard   Focus reticule   Exposure reticule   Zoom controls and presets

2.10 FiLMiC Pro on the iPhone

Focus Lock   Exposure Lock   White Balance Lock   Torch (flash)   Library   Settings   Record

Just this one feature can dramatically improve the quality of your clips. Unlike the single control in the Camera app, which sets focus and exposure at the same location, FiLMiC Pro can let you focus on one subject while using another area to calculate exposure.

Drag the square Focus reticule onto the area you want to remain sharp (2.11), and drag the circular Exposure reticule to the area to be used as a base for lighting. You can drag each control simultaneously using a finger for each. The Focus reticule requires a second for the app to adjust focus, but the Exposure reticule adjusts the lighting as you drag. In general, placing the Exposure control over a dark area makes a scene brighter and placing it on a bright area makes the scene darker.

The focus and exposure are adjustable while you're recording, too. To lock them, tap the appropriate lock button (which then turns red) at the bottom of the screen.

2.11 Focusing on a different subject

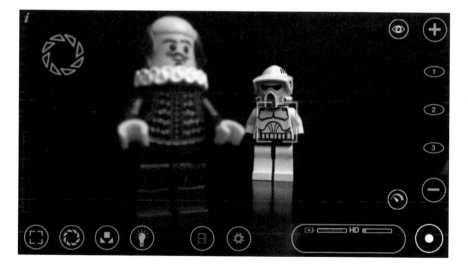

▶ **TIP** FiLMiC Pro also offers a single reticule that incorporates both focus and exposure if you prefer. Tap the Settings button, scroll down and tap Reticule, and then choose either Single; Fixed or Single; or Movable.

▶ **TIP** Even if your iPhone or iPad is mounted on a tripod and pointed at a subject that isn't going to move, lock the focus and exposure before recording. The image will bounce a little as the device continually attempts to focus, and small lighting changes in the scene (such as clouds) can adjust the exposure in a distracting way.

The third lock button controls white balance (the color temperature of the scene), even though FiLMiC Pro doesn't include a specific white balance control. It will automatically determine the color balance of a scene, but you can help it out: Hold a white sheet of paper in front of the camera and then tap the White Balance Lock button. As with locking focus, it's a good idea to nail down the white balance before shooting to avoid unexpected automatic color shifts while you're recording.

Zoom Control

As I mentioned earlier, I'm not a fan of digital zoom. Because the iPhone and iPad cameras don't have separate moving lens elements that optically enlarge the image, the devices rely on software to simulate the effect. The result is degraded image quality, because the processor is adding pixels based on an algorithm instead of recording them in real life.

That said, the zoom feature in FiLMiC Pro is pretty cool. If you're not in a position where you can physically move the device, you can simulate a push-camera move in the app.

To zoom in, either before you begin to record or during filming, touch and hold the + button until you've reached the desired level of zoom. A red bar—vertical on the iPhone, horizontal on the iPad (2.12)—indicates the amount.

2.12 Zoom controls on the iPad

Zoom/Zoom Speed toggle   Zoom indicator   Zoom Out   Zoom In

Zoom speed

FiLMiC Pro also includes a way to control the speed of the zoom. Did you ever fight with the rocker switches used for zooming on camcorders? Nudge the switch a little and the zoom is barely perceptible, but hit it too hard and suddenly the camera is focused on someone's nose hairs. You can choose how fast or slow the zoom happens.

Tap the Zoom/Zoom Speed toggle button to view the current speed setting, which appears in green in the zoom indicator bar. Tap the Zoom Out or Zoom In button to change the speed (2.13).

2.13 Setting zoom speed on the iPad

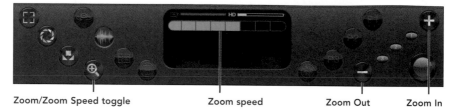

Zoom/Zoom Speed toggle   Zoom speed   Zoom Out   Zoom In

Zoom presets

An added benefit—and really, what makes this feature nifty—is the ability to set up to three zoom presets. Instead of holding the + or – button and hoping you hit the right level (especially if you're shooting multiple takes of a scene), determine at the outset where those points will be. Let's say you want the camera to zoom in halfway to the maximum amount, then zoom out to about 25 percent, and finally zoom out to normal. Here's how:

1. Press the + button until the red bar reaches about halfway to the top. (This sequence is easier to achieve if the camera is stationary on a tripod or other support.)

2. Touch and hold the 1 button in the zoom controls. A small indicator with a single red dot appears within the red bar.

3. Press the – button to zoom out until the level is about a quarter of the size of the full bar.

4. Touch and hold the 2 button. An indicator with two red dots appears.

5. Press the – button to zoom entirely out.

6. Touch and hold the 3 button until a third indicator appears (2.14).

2.14 Zoom presets configured on the iPhone

Zoom preset number 3

When it's time to record, tap (but don't hold) the 1 button. FiLMiC Pro smoothly zooms to the halfway mark and stops (2.15). Similarly, tap the 2 button to zoom out slightly, and then tap the 3 button when you want to zoom completely out.

2.15 Zoomed halfway and stopped on the number 2 preset

To remove a preset, touch and hold the number button until the indicator disappears from the zoom amount bar.

Remember, the zoom feature is digital, so you'll see lower image quality as you zoom in closer. However, using the feature in moderation can add motion to a scene without much visible difference.

Recording Speed

With the Camera app, all of the recording settings are baked in. If you've delved at all into video, though, you know that a myriad of speeds, formats, and data rates are possible. FiLMiC Pro exposes many of those alternatives, enabling you to shoot video that plays back in slow motion (even if you don't own an iPhone 5s) or accelerated speed, and at different frames-per-second rates. The app offers many presets for switching speeds, as well as the ability to create your own presets. And if you're particularly picky about the result, or you expect to edit the footage in a desktop application such as Final Cut Pro X, you can change the overall quality of the footage (at the expense of device storage).

Choose a recording speed

iMovie and other video editors can speed up or slow down your video during editing, but it's a bit of a cheat. The app either adds frames that weren't present originally to slow the footage, or removes frames to speed it up.

As you learned earlier in this chapter, the way to shoot slow-motion footage is to capture more frames; the iPhone 5s records 120 frames per second in its Slo-Mo mode. Conversely, to make action appear to move faster than normal, you capture fewer frames.

Tap the Settings button to access the app's presets, and then tap a speed preset to activate it (2.16).

2.16 FiLMiC Pro's many speed options

FiLMiC Pro v58	Settings					Close

Presets

Standard Sync Audio

24	25	30

Fast Capture 720

48	50	60	120

Accelerated Motion FX

2x (12/24)	3x (8/24)	4x (6/24)	6x (4/24)	8x (3/24)	12x (2/24)	24x (2/48)	60x (2/120)

Slow Motion FX

30/24	36/24	48/24	60/24	120/24	60/6	120/6

At first glance, the settings appear to be written in a secret code, but here's the translation:

- Standard Sync Audio is the frame rate at which to capture the video while preserving the audio. Video is normally shot at 30 fps, whereas movies projected in theaters are shot at 24 or 25 fps. Since FiLMiC Pro is mostly geared toward independent filmmakers, its default is 24 fps. This setting is really based on your personal preference, as each one creates a different look.

- The Fast Capture 720 options are those that FiLMiC Pro can activate using the camera's default capabilities. (The screenshot above was taken on an iPhone 5s; other devices lack the 120 option.)

- The Accelerated Motion FX and Slow Motion FX options rely on the device's GPU (graphics processing unit) to achieve the speeds.

- The "x" is the multiplier, so "4x (6/24)" is video that plays back four times as fast as normal.

- The other numbers represent the capture frame rate and the playback frame rate. So, "4x (6/24)" is video played at four times normal, captured at 6 fps and played back at 24 fps. The Slow Motion FX option "60/24," therefore, captures 60 fps and plays back at 24 fps.

If you need to use different frame rates, or want to easily combine features that aren't activated in one of the FiLMiC Pro presets, you can create your own. Tap a custom preset button (such as C1), and scroll down the Settings screen to find specific settings (2.17).

For example, let's say you want to shoot 720p (1280x720) to save some storage on your device, and you also want the video captured at 30 fps and the Zoom capability to be off. The next time you tap C1, those settings are enabled.

2.17 Plenty of FiLMiC Pro settings

▶ **TIP** In addition to 720p and 1080p, the Resolution options include "1280x720 iFrame" and "960x540 iFrame." iFrame is a format that is optimized to work especially well with iMovie on the Mac. If you're shooting with the expectation to edit on the Mac later, consider the 1280x720 HD option (960x540 is standard definition).

Video bit rates and audio quality

Here's another reason advanced photographers like to shoot video with FiLMiC Pro: The app can record in higher quality than what Apple offers in the Camera app. In this case, quality is measured not in resolution but in bit rate—the amount of data that's recorded per second.

The app's default, FiLMiC Quality, is 32 mbit/sec (megabits per second)—which is higher than Apple's standard 24 mbit/sec. You can also tap into FiLMiC Extreme at 50 mbit/sec for the highest quality. In real terms, that means less compression and more raw data to play with, which is helpful if you're editing on the desktop using something like Final Cut Pro X, where you'll potentially be adjusting the color.

As for audio, you can't magically replace the iPhone or iPad microphones, which record only in mono, but you can choose a quality level and whether the audio is compressed or uncompressed. The default is 48 khz compressed (AAC encoding), which you can knock down to 44.1 khz, or switch to uncompressed 44.1 khz or 48 khz (Linear PCM encoding).

Other Helpful FiLMiC Pro Features

Okay, you can tell that FiLMiC Pro has more to offer than the Camera app. And yet there are a bunch of other features that can help you shoot. For example, open Settings and explore these options:

- Image Stabilization is off by default, but if you're filming handheld and want to take the shaking edge off your video, turn the option on. However, note that it's particularly battery intensive and it heats up the phone.

- The Mode setting offers an Efficiency Mode that doesn't require the GPU for effects, which results in longer battery life and less heat.

- Turning on the Thirds Guide overlay displays a rule-of-thirds grid to help you compose your scenes. The Thirds Guide button on the main screen on the iPad also toggles this option without requiring a trip to the Settings screen.

- A Matte overlay option imposes black bars to force an aspect ratio such as 2.35:1 (cinematic wide angle). However, I recommend ignoring Matte and turn on the Framing Guide overlay instead, which displays guidelines to mark the visible area. That way, you're not deliberately cutting out material during the recording phase; let the editing soft-ware (and this option applies to projects edited on the computer) do it for you later.

- The Header options display a slate before you record each clip, with the information you provide, such as director, project, and scene (2.18).

- The Content Management options let you specify how the clips are named, including information about the project, scene, and take.

2.18 Optionally include a slate that appears in front of each take.

Exporting Videos from FiLMiC Pro

Clips you record from FiLMiC Pro are saved within the app. To make them available to an editing app such as iMovie, do the following:

1. Tap the Library button to view the list of recorded clips.

2. Tap the Edit button and then choose the clips you want to export.

3. Tap the Copy To Camera Roll button to create copies in the Camera Roll. Those can now be imported into other applications.

▶ **TIP** This book focuses on editing on the device itself, but if your footage is meant to be edited on a computer, you'll need to pass it through iTunes first. Select a clip from the list, tap the Share button, and choose iTunes from the list that appears. The next time you connect the device to your computer, you can transfer the clip from within iTunes (see Chapter 7).

Another Step Up: Ultrakam

FiLMiC Pro is a big leap up from the built-in Camera app, but a new app called Ultrakam4K wants to increase the quality and resolution of the video. Ultrakam4K ties into the still-photo capabilities of the device's camera to shoot at up to 3K resolution (2592 x 1936) (or export to YouTube at "4K Quality"). A separate Ultrakam Pro app also captures raw footage—what the camera is recording, without conversion and compression.

ZeroShake

FiLMiC Pro includes an image stabilization feature, but what if you know you'll be shooting a situation that's guaranteed to jostle the camera around? ZeroShake is simple to use and does a good job of making your viewers think you glide on glass everywhere.

1. The first thing to do when opening the app is to tap the Settings button and change the video resolution to 720p or 1080p instead of the default, standard-definition 480p.

2. Tap the ZeroShake button to set the amount of stabilization to apply.

3. Tap the red Record button to start capturing video. As you shoot, keep the crosshairs in the middle box and the red level indicator at left between the black bars (2.19).

2.19 Recording in ZeroShake

8mm

Moving about as far away from the polish of FiLMiC Pro as you can, 8mm is designed to achieve nearly the opposite effect: the 8-millimeter movies of old (8mm was the width of the film). Or, rather, the way 8mm films look today, with all the film grain, light leaks, and jitter that they entail.

Switch between several presets, such as 70s, Indigo, and Noir; change the simulated lens; and tap the big red metal button to start recording (2.20). The Frame Jitter button in the lower-right corner slips the "film" to add grungy character to the clip. You can also import footage that you shot with other apps and process them using the 8mm filters (2.21).

2.20 8mm

2.21 Video shot with the Camera app and converted in 8mm

Horizon

Earlier I oh-so-subtly hinted that perhaps people should never, ever shoot video with the iPhone or iPad in its portrait (tall) orientation. And yet, especially with phones, I see people do it all the time.

Now look, I'm not disparaging people who do this. I also no longer look askance at folks shooting photos or video on the iPad—what at first seemed completely odd is now becoming commonplace based on my experience. The issue with shooting video horizontally is one of quality; doing so throws away valuable footage.

The developers of Horizon must have thought the same thing, because this clever app will capture horizontal video no matter how you hold the device. It uses the accelerometer in the iPhone or iPad to determine the device's orientation and compensates to maintain a horizontal aspect ratio (2.22).

The downside is that the footage appears to zoom in and out as its borders are cropped to accommodate the motion. To get around that, tap the Mode button (at the upper-left corner in the figure below) and switch from Rotate & Scale to just Rotate.

2.22 Horizon

Recorded result

Area being captured

iPhone held at jaunty angle

Instagram and Vine Videos

In general, the approach of this book assumes that you're capturing video clips and then editing them into a longer piece. But what if you want to snag just a few seconds of footage to share a quick idea or mood? Both Instagram and Vine make this task incredibly easy. The videos are limited to a set time—15 seconds for Instagram, 6 seconds for Vine—which gives you creative restriction to work with. I'll use Instagram as the example, but both apps work similarly.

1. In the Instagram app, tap the Video button (which looks like a video camera) to switch to video mode.

2. Touch and hold the big red Record button to start recording. The blue progress bar indicates how much time you've used (2.23).

2.23 Capturing an Instagram movie. The app's interface is designed for portrait orientation, but I was holding the camera in horizontal orientation.

3. Lift your finger to stop recording.

4. Touch and hold the Record button again to shoot the next consecutive clip. If you don't like the previous section, tap the Delete button.

5. Continue adding clips until the limit is reached, or tap the Next button to continue.

6. Choose a filter (if you want one) and then tap Next.

7. Drag to scroll through the filmstrip at the bottom of the screen to choose which frame appears as the movie's cover (2.24). Tap Next.

2.24 Choose a cover frame (left) and share the finished video (right).

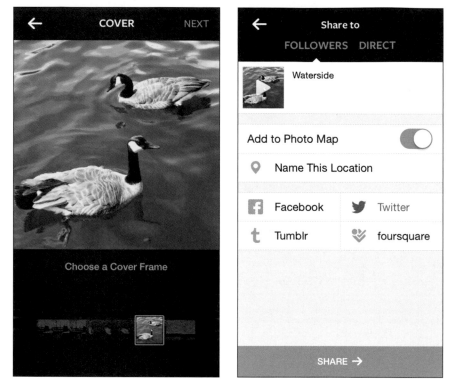

8. Instagram videos and photos are posted to your Instagram feed, which means that only people who already subscribe to your photos will see the movie. On the Share To screen, you can also opt to share via Facebook, Twitter, Tumblr, or Foursquare.

9. Tap Share to finish.

▶ **TIP** One advantage Vine has over Instagram is the ability to lightly edit your movie before it's posted. After capturing your clips, tap the Edit button. You can drag the clips to rearrange them, or drag them to the trash icon to delete them.

▶ **TIP** In a similar vein, check out an app called Flashback. As you're shooting, it acts like a still-photo camera. Tap the shutter and it snaps a picture. But behind the scenes, it's recording video and saving 5 seconds of footage.

Shoot Using a GoPro

If you thought the iPhone was the ultimate expression of a go-anywhere camera, the GoPro puts it to shame. Essentially an HD camcorder built within a tiny box, GoPro cameras are small enough to mount nearly anywhere. Extreme sports, auto races, underwater dives—if it looks like an impossible shot, a GoPro probably captured it. When I went zip-lining one day in Hawaii, in fact, the company running the course already had a helmet equipped with a GoPro mount.

So what does this have to do with the iPhone or iPad? The GoPro has no viewfinder or LCD screen, and it's often mounted in places that may not be easy to reach. Using the GoPro app for iOS, however, you can control the GoPro's settings and playback, transfer its video clips to the iPhone or iPad, and edit the footage.

Set Up the GoPro

I must admit, one of the appeals of using the GoPro app is being able to adjust any of its settings without having to navigate the in-camera menu system. It's much easier to adjust the resolution by tapping an option on the iPhone than by pressing multiple buttons on the GoPro itself.

The iOS device connects to the GoPro via Wi-Fi. Here's how to set up the connection:

1. On the GoPro, press the Wi-Fi button on the side.

2. On the iOS device, go to Settings > Wi-Fi and choose the name of the GoPro. (If you haven't set up a password yet, try the default, "goprohero".)

3. Open the GoPro app.

4. Tap the Connect + Control button (2.25).

▶   **TIP** Fair warning: Keeping Wi-Fi acitve on the GoPro makes the battery drain faster.

2.25 Connect to a GoPro.

Set Up iOS-Friendly Video Settings

The GoPro is an incredibly sophisticated camera, capable of shooting up to 4K resolution in the latest models, but not everything transfers cleanly to iOS. So, the first thing you must decide is whether you want to trade off image quality and editing flexibility.

Since this book is focused on working entirely on iOS devices, I'm assuming you're okay with shooting video in less-than-optimal formats. And let me be clear: We're still talking about 1080p HD footage, so you're not really suffering. But if you want to take full advantage of what the GoPro can capture, you'll need to transfer the footage to a Mac or a Windows PC and convert the video there.

Do the following to ensure you can work with the video on your device.

1. Tap the Settings button (marked by a wrench icon) to access the Settings screen (2.26).

2. Under Camera Settings, set Video Resolution to 1080, 960, or 720.

3. If you've shot other footage in a specific frame rate, such as 24 fps, then match it in the Frame Rate option.

4. Set the Field of View to Wide, Medium, or Narrow, depending on the look you want.

5. Under Capture Settings, turn Protune off. Protune is what enables additional settings such as White Balance, but footage saved with Protune enabled can't be read by the iPhone or iPad.

6. Tap Done to return to the camera control screen.

Settings	Done
CAMERA SETTINGS	
Video Resolution	1080 >
Frame Rate	60 FPS >
Field of View	MEDIUM >
Photo Resolution	12MP WIDE >

2.26 GoPro settings

Control the GoPro

After you tap the Connect + Control button on the app's main screen, you're presented with the interface to control the camera (2.27). A live preview shows you what the GoPro is seeing (with a noticeable lag), which is helpful when you're composing your shot. You can also tap the preview area to switch to a larger view; rotating the device provides a larger wide-screen view (2.28), and tapping the screen once hides the controls.

To start capturing video, tap the red Record button. Tap it again to stop.

2.27 Control the GoPro.

2.28 Widescreen preview

Import Footage from the GoPro

When you've finished shooting, the clips are stored on the GoPro's memory card; the GoPro app is just a window to the video. To make them available to other apps, such as iMovie, you must first import them from the GoPro into the Camera Roll on the iPad or iPhone.

1. At the GoPro control screen, tap the Media button (which has a grid of four boxes) to open the GoPro Media screen (**2.29**).

2. Tap the Edit button.

3. Tap to select the clips you want to import.

4. Tap the Share button.

5. Tap the GoPro Album button that appears.

6. Choose which resolution to copy. Low Resolution is good for throwing together a quick edit without swamping your device's storage.

2.29 Recorded clips

The imported clips are transferred to the iPhone or iPad and saved to the Camera Roll. From there you can import them into iMovie or another editor.

CHAPTER 3

Edit Video

Video is magic. The brain interprets a succession of still frames as motion, and even though we know that the action in a video clip isn't "real," to some degree we believe that it is. We empathize with the characters, marvel at the locations, and follow the story—no matter the content, documentary or fiction. A child playing outside can be just as compelling as a science fiction adventure, and at no point do we say, "Look at how those 30 frames are working together every second."

When you combine clips, though, another level of magic takes place. You can tell stories that don't fit into a single clip, enhance or suppress emotions by choosing scenes (or just parts of scenes), and often discover serendipitous mixtures of video, audio, and timing that elevate the footage you captured.

And let's not forget that all of this happens on the sleek rectangle in your hands. Editing video used to be possible only on large, expensive desktop computers. Now, using iMovie or apps like Pinnacle Studio, you can do it all on the iPhone or iPad.

Before we start splicing clips, though, I want to start with a couple of apps that can improve your footage in preparation for editing.

Stabilize Footage with Emulsio

In Chapter 2, I spotlighted ZeroShake as a tool to prevent shaky video. The only problem with that approach is that you need to expect, before you record, that you'll be shooting shaky footage. More often, you'll use the Camera app or FiLMiC Pro and only later realize that the footage isn't as stable as you'd like.

Emulsio is a great pre-editing app that analyzes a video clip and determines how to zoom and position the image to avoid or minimize camera shake.

1. Open the Emulsio app.

2. Tap a video you want to stabilize. Emulsio analyzes the clip.

3. Tap the Play button to view the stabilized clip.

4. Tap the Live Comparison button to see how much stabilization has been applied (3.1). To get a geeky insight into what Emulsio is doing, tap the Stabilizer Data Reporting button, which reveals (as the video plays) the amount of displacement used to achieve the stability (3.2).

3.1 Comparing original (left) and stabilized (right) video in Emulsio

3.2 Stabilizer Data Reporting view (on iPhone)

5. If the video is still too shaky, adjust the Stabilization Strength slider at right. You can also change or disable specific types of compensation by tapping the buttons at left: Translation Compensation (the direction the camera moves) in the X, Y, or XY axes; Rotation Compensation (how the camera was turned); and Wobble Removal (counteracting the jelly appearance that can be caused by the rolling shutter).

6. If you want, drag the selection handles in the filmstrip at the top of the screen to trim the footage.

7. Tap the Pause button to stop playback.

8. Tap the Share button to export the stabilized footage.

9. In the share sheet that appears, tap Save Video to store the clip in the Camera Roll.

► **TIP** Stabilization is achieved by zooming in on the image so it can be shifted or rotated without visible borders appearing. The higher the Stabilization Strength setting, the more cropped the image appears **(3.3)**.

50% stabilization

100% stabilization

3.3 Stabilization amounts

Adjust Color in VideoGrade

When you capture a still photo, you know there are many options for adjusting the color and tone later in case the shot doesn't look quite right. To perform those types of edits on video footage, turn to VideoGrade. (*Color grading* is the movie industry term for adjusting colors during post-production. Some movies employ sweeping color grading to change the overall appearance of the film; think of *O Brother, Where Art Thou?* and its faded sepia tone as one example.)

1. In VideoGrade, choose a clip from the albums and events in the device's Camera Roll.

2. Using the controls at the bottom of the screen, adjust up to 11 attributes of the video. For example, to warm a cloudy scene, tap the Temperature button and choose a white balance preset (3.4) or tap the gear icon and choose a temperature by dragging the slider.

3.4 Adjusting color temperature in VideoGrade

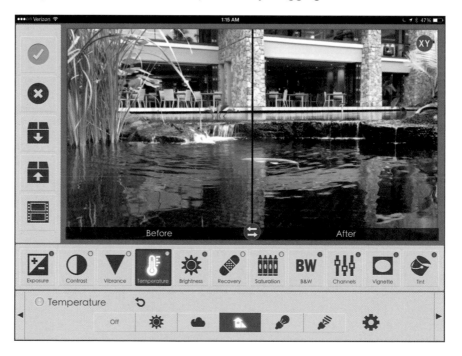

3. Tap the Filmstrip button to scroll through the video and see how the adjustments apply to any frame. You can also trim the clip here.

> ► **TIP** In the filmstrip mode, tap the camera button to save a frame as a still image to the Camera Roll. This option is a good way to share the look of the video with someone without sending the entire graded video file.

4. Tap the green checkmark when you're ready to export the adjusted movie.

5. In the Export Options screen, optionally change the resolution, frame rate, and quality. Tap the green Play button to continue. After a few minutes (depending on the length of the video), the footage is converted and added to the Camera Roll.

That's impressive enough, but what makes VideoGrade truly useful is the ability to save the settings as a preset, and then load the preset later for other clips.

1. Adjust the settings to get the look you want.

2. Tap the Save Preset button (the box with the down-facing arrow).

3. Type a name for the preset.

4. Open a new clip and tap the Load Preset button.

5. Choose the preset you saved (3.5).

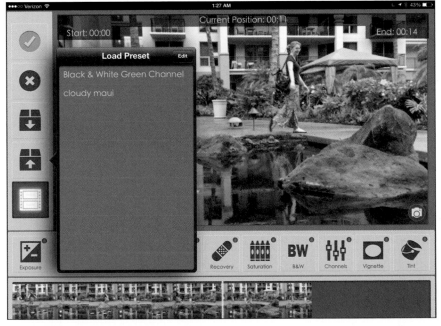

3.5 Apply presets to other clips.

Edit Video in iMovie

This chapter focuses mostly on iMovie because it's one of the easiest ways to edit video (while still wielding a lot of power) and because it's free to anyone who buys a new iOS device; if you do find yourself needing to pony up some cash for the app, it'll set you back only $4.99.

Initially iMovie was a fairly basic video editor, but its latest incarnation is surprisingly sophisticated. Whether you're tossing together a quick sequence or editing a longer piece, iMovie continues to chip at that false idea that "mobile" equals "less capable."

Review and Mark Clips

As you build up a library of video clips and start editing them, you'll want to find the quality ones in a way that's easier than constantly scrolling. You can mark an entire clip or just portions of a clip as favorites in iMovie's Video view, and then display just those clips later when editing.

1. Open iMovie and tap the Video button at the top of the screen, if it's not already active.

2. Tap a video clip to display a large preview (3.6).

3. In addition to playing the clip, you can review it at fast speed (tap the bunny) or slow speed (tap the turtle).

3.6 Previewing a video clip

4. Drag the selection handles at the start and end of the clip to define a good selection, if you wish.

5. Tap the heart button to mark the clip or the section as a favorite.

▶ **TIP** Tap the Favorites button as the clip is playing to mark 4-second increments.

▶ **TIP** iMovie looks to the device's photo library for video clips. It's often helpful to group related clips (such as from a vacation) into a new album to make it easier to locate them while editing.

Create a Trailer

When Apple introduced this feature, I thought it was...cute. Instead of starting from scratch to cut a movie together, you can drop clips into pre-made templates. Trailers are fun, but more important, they quickly help someone new to video editing create a short movie and learn the basics of the process.

1. In iMovie, tap the Projects button at the top of the screen.

2. Tap the + button to create a new project.

3. Tap the Trailer button.

4. Choose a template and preview it by tapping the Play button (3.7). The description below the preview area of some templates indicates the number of people (cast members) the trailer is designed for.

3.7 Trailer template preview

5. Tap the Create Trailer button to use the selected template.

6. In the Outline view, type a title in the Movie Name field and fill out the rest of the fields (3.8). You can also choose a logo style for your fictional studio name.

3.8 Create your own credits.

7. Tap the Storyboard tab. The first scene placeholder is selected.

8. Scroll through your video clips to find one that matches the type of shot (such as Landscape, Wide, or Action).

9. Tap the clip; iMovie highlights a section that's the duration needed for the placeholder. Drag to find the section you want to use, and then tap the Add to Project button (3.9).

3.9 Choosing a clip to use in a shot

Selected shot   Add to Project   Preview Clip

10. To change the text that appears between scenes, tap the text fields between scenes and type your own words.

11. Add clips to the rest of the scenes.

12. To use a different portion of a clip in a scene, tap the shot and, in the Edit Shot area, drag to reposition the frame within the clip (3.10). You can also tap the trash can button to delete the clip and choose another.

3.10 Editing a shot

13. Tap the Play in Viewer or Play Full Screen button to watch the trailer.

14. Tap the Back button (<) to return to the project view.

▶ **TIP** Clips are automatically muted so they don't conflict with the trailers' soundtracks (which are professionally recorded), but you can un-mute them. Tap a shot to select it, and in the Edit Shot area, tap the volume icon to turn off the mute setting. Tap Done to apply the change.

Transfer Clips Between Devices

iMovie works the same on all iOS devices, but I prefer to shoot using the iPhone and edit using the iPad's bigger screen. That combination presents a problem: What's the best way to transfer video clips from one device to the other? iOS offers two methods that both work.

If you're using modern models (iPhone 5 or later, fourth-generation iPad and later, and fifth-generation iPod touch), AirDrop can send clips wirelessly. Make sure both devices are unlocked and do the following:

1. On the source device, which contains the clips, open the Photos app and go to the Camera Roll or the Videos album.

2. Tap the Select button.

3. Choose one or more clips to share.

4. Tap the Share button. The destination device's name should appear in the AirDrop area of the share sheet.

5. Tap the name of the device you want to send the file(s) to.

6. On the destination device, agree to receive the files, which begins the transfer.

This approach works well for one or two clips, but isn't ideal for more than that due to the large sizes of the video files. A better option in that case is to transfer the clips via USB, using Apple's Lightning to USB Camera Adapter or the USB component of the Camera Connection Kit (for iPads with 30-pin ports); this only works when moving clips from an iPhone to an iPad, however.

1. Connect the adapter to the destination iPad.

2. Plug the sync cable that came with the iPhone or iPad between the USB slot of the adapter and the iPhone.

3. Open the Photos app on the destination iPad.

4. Tap the Import button.

5. Select the videos you want, and tap the Import button at the top of the screen. The clips transfer just as if they were photos.

USB connections are much faster than wireless, so the files copy quickly between devices.

Create a Movie

Trailers are fun, but you're locked into a rigid template. When you create a Movie project instead, you have free rein over editing video, photos, and audio clips.

1. Tap the Projects button to open the Projects browser.

2. Tap the Create Project (+) button and choose Movie.

3. Choose a theme (tap the triangular Play button to preview its appearance) and then tap the Create Movie button.

   Every movie must have a theme. You won't see evidence of the theme unless you specifically choose a themed transition or add a title to a clip. You can also change a project's theme at any time. Any themed assets in the movie automatically switch to the chosen theme (which means you can't mix and match elements from different themes).

4. iMovie takes you to the editing environment (3.11), which works in either the horizontal or portrait orientation.

Viewer   Media Library

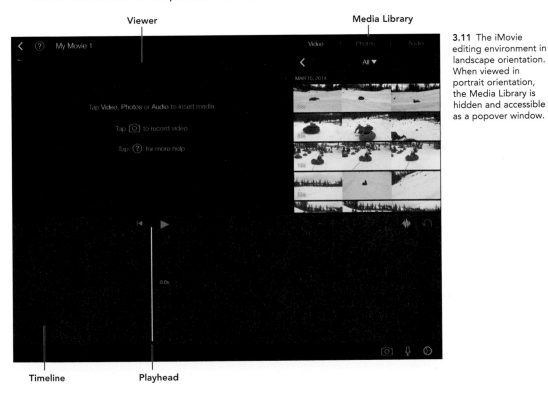

3.11 The iMovie editing environment in landscape orientation. When viewed in portrait orientation, the Media Library is hidden and accessible as a popover window.

Timeline   Playhead

▶ **TIP** If you create a project and then immediately return to the opening screen, iMovie discards the new project because it has no content.

▶ **TIP** On the iPad, the Viewer doesn't need to be on the left side. If you're left-handed or you just prefer that the Viewer and Media Library swap places, drag the top of the Viewer or Media Library to the other side.

Add Clips from the Media Library

The process of editing is accretive: add clips, or portions of clips, to the project's timeline to build a full movie. That, of course, begins with the raw video content.

1. Scroll to the position in the timeline where you want the clip to appear. (This doesn't apply if no clips are in the timeline yet.)

2. On an iPhone or when holding an iPad in its portrait orientation, tap the Media Library button. If you're editing on the iPad in landscape orientation, the Media Library appears in the upper-right corner.

3. If you marked favorite clips or sections in the Video browser (described earlier in this chapter), tap the down-facing triangle at the top of the Media Library and tap Favorites (3.12). You can also browse your clips by album by tapping the Back button (<) at the top of the library.

3.12 Editing a shot

4. To preview the contents of a clip, touch and hold briefly and then drag your finger across it.

5. Tap once on a clip to reveal its selection handles.

6. To add just a portion of the clip, drag the handles to define it (3.13). You can also tap the gray Play button to review just the selected range.

7. Tap the Add button (the arrow) to add the clip to the timeline. (The ellipses button reveals controls for adding a cutaway, picture-in-picture, side-by-side, or audio-only clip. I cover those options later in the chapter.)

▶ **TIP** You can rearrange videos all you want in iMovie, so don't feel as if you need to establish the movie's order yet. Some people prefer to toss the clips they intend to use on the timeline and then sort it out.

3.13 Select a portion of a video clip to add.

Capture Video Directly

Using the cameras on the iPad, you can record video directly into your iMovie timeline. However, iMovie treats video differently depending on whether it was captured or imported: Video shot in iMovie stays within iMovie; it isn't automatically added to the Camera Roll. If you create a new project, that clip you shot in a previous project won't appear at all. However, there is a way to make the clip available to all projects.

With a project open, do the following:

1. Tap the Camera button.

2. Set the mode switch to video.

3. Tap the Record button to begin capturing the footage.

4. Tap the Record button again to stop recording.

5. Press the Play button to review your footage. If the clip is acceptable, tap the Use Video button; the clip appears in the Video browser and at the point in your movie where the playhead was positioned. If the clip isn't what you want, tap the Retake button and shoot again.

To make the video available to other projects and apps, do this:

1. Tap the disclosure triangle at the top of the Media Library.

2. Choose "Manage local media."

3. Select the clip recorded in iMovie and tap the Save to Camera Roll button.

Play and Skim Video

The timeline in iMovie for iOS runs left to right across the bottom of the screen. Tap the Play button to preview the movie in real time in the Viewer.

To skim the timeline, swipe left or right. Or, tap the Reverse button to the left of the Play button to jump back to previous edit marks (the control doesn't appear in the iPhone's landscape view, though). The playhead remains stationary, so instead of positioning the playhead on the video, you're actually moving the video clips under the playhead (3.14).

3.14 The Viewer shows the current frame under the playhead.

▶ **TIP** When the video clips expand beyond the edges of the screen, touch and hold the upper-left edge of the timeline to quickly jump to the beginning of the movie. Hold the upper-right edge to jump to the end.

▶ **NOTE** I must share two frustrations with the Media Library. When you exit iMovie to do something else and then return, the app lists all movies instead of the album you were working in. Also, the Album view lists all albums alphabetically—even events that are listed by date. So if you want to access clips from your vacation to Zimbabwe, you need to scroll all the way to the bottom of the list after reopening iMovie. Although this is a clunky workaround, consider going to the Photos app and renaming an album with "0" or "a" at the start to make it appear at the top of the list.

▶ **TIP** To view more thumbnails in the timeline, pinch outward horizontally with two fingers; pinch inward to view fewer thumbnails.

Move a Clip on the Timeline

As editor, you have the power to arrange clips however you want.

1. Touch and hold the clip you want to move. It lifts out of the timeline as a small thumbnail (3.15).

2. Without lifting your finger from the screen, drag the clip to a new location in the timeline.

3.15 Move a clip in the timeline.

After move

Trim a Clip

You can select a portion of a clip when you import it, but you'll also find yourself trimming clips to fine-tune their timing.

1. Tap a clip once to reveal its selection handles (the yellow edges).

2. Drag a handle to shorten or lengthen a clip (3.16).

3.16 Trim a clip.

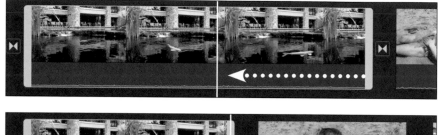

Split a Clip

Sometimes you want to split a clip to use a section elsewhere in the movie; perhaps you kept recording after one event and managed to catch another great moment a short while later. In that case, you can hark back to the editing days of old, and slice the clip as if you'd taken a razor to film.

1. Position the clip so the playhead is at the point where you want to split it.

2. Tap the clip to select it.

3. Tap the Split button at the bottom of the screen. Or, slide one finger down the playhead from the top of the clip to the bottom (3.17). The clip is split into two, with a transition added between them. (The transition, however, is set to None, so there's no break between clips when you play the video. See "Edit Transitions," later in the chapter.)

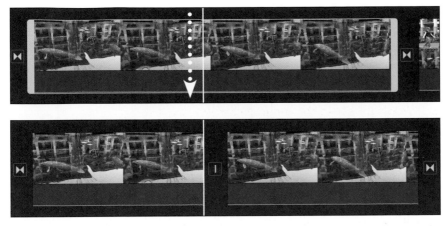

3.17 Split a clip.

▶ **TIP** If you're looking to drop footage into the middle of a clip that's already on the timeline, you may be better off adding a cutaway instead of splitting the clip. I discuss cutaways a few pages ahead.

Duplicate a Clip

Here's another secret of editing video: You can re-use clips. Sometimes that could be to emphasize something by repeating it. Maybe you're constructing your own *Rashomon* movie that examines an event from multiple viewpoints. Or perhaps you want to use another section of a longer clip without having to find it again in the Media Library.

Whatever the case, it's easy to duplicate a clip on the timeline. Tap to select the clip, and then tap the Duplicate button at the bottom of the screen. On the iPhone, tap the button farthest to the right to reveal additional editing commands, including Duplicate (3.18).

3.18 Duplicate command

Tap to reveal more commands

Reframe a Clip

One of the most frequently used edits in still photography is reframing (cropping) an image to change composition. In iMovie you can zoom in and reposition the clip within the frame to achieve the same effect.

1. Tap to select the clip you want to edit.

2. Tap the Zoom Control button (the magnifying glass) in the lower-right corner of the Viewer.

3. Pinch with two fingers to zoom in on the image.

4. Drag with one finger to reposition it within the frame.

5. Tap the Zoom Control button again; or, tap outside the clip to deselect it and apply the change (3.19).

To restore the clip to its original framing, tap the Zoom Control button and then double-tap the Viewer.

3.19 Zoom in on a clip.

Original framing

Adjusted framing

Remove a Clip

The easy way to remove a clip from the timeline is to select it and then tap the trash can button at the bottom of the screen. But why do that when you can make it vanish in a puff of smoke? Drag a clip from the timeline to the Viewer until you see a small cloud icon appear, and then lift your finger (3.20). Deleting clips only removes them from your movie; they're still present in the Media Library.

3.20 Removing a clip

Add a Cutaway, Picture-in-Picture, or Split-Screen Overlay

A movie is linear, and iMovie lines up clips one after another on the timeline. But you're not limited to playing just one clip at a time. You may want to highlight two things happening at the same time, or cut to a second clip while the audio from the original clip continues to play. That's where iMovie's clip overlays come into play.

Cutaway

A cutaway shot is so common you may not even notice it. Typically, action is happening onscreen in one clip, but you want to switch the visual to something else without breaking up the first one. For example, during a recent vacation my daughter and I stopped to watch a woodcarver work. I captured video of him carving, but also made a point of shooting some footage of my daughter watching the work. I want to cut between the two clips, but use only the audio from the woodcarver's clip.

If only one layer of video were available, I'd have to slice and dice the clips. Instead, a cutaway accomplishes the effect quickly and easily.

1. Add the clip you want to act as a base. Cutaways can only be added on top of existing clips.

2. Position the playhead over the frame where you want the cutaway to begin. (Don't worry, you can adjust its location later if needed.)

3. In the Media Library, select the clip to use as the cutaway (3.21).

4. Tap the Cutaway button. The clip appears on top of the video on the timeline (3.22).

▶ **TIP** The audio for both clips will play simultaneously, so you'll probably want to mute the cutaway: Select it, tap the Audio button at the bottom of the screen, and drag the volume slider to zero or tap the speaker icon.

A cutaway clip (and any overlay appearing above the timeline's base layer) can be trimmed, split, and dragged horizontally for best placement.

3.21 Add a cutaway

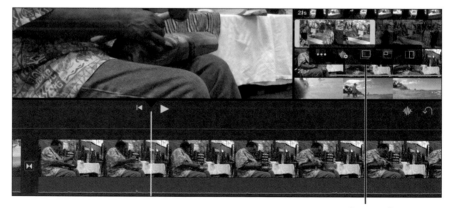

Cutaway button

3.22 Cutaway added above the original clip

Picture-in-picture

A picture-in-picture effect works especially well in situations where you want to show two things happening at the same time (great if you shot footage using two devices, such as an iPhone and a GoPro). Or, in a more traditional approach, it can illustrate what someone onscreen (such as a news anchor or reporter) is discussing.

Perform the same steps as for adding a cutaway, but tap the Picture-in-Picture button instead of the Cutaway button. The clip appears above the base clip in the timeline.

Once you've applied the picture-in-picture clip, you can adjust its size and placement within the frame.

1. Tap the clip in the timeline to select it.

2. In the Viewer, tap the Position Control button in the lower-right corner (just above the magnifying glass).

3. Pinch with two fingers to change the size of the picture. To reposition it, drag with one finger (3.23).

4. Tap the Position Control button again to apply the change.

3.23 Move and resize the picture-in-picture effect.

Position Control button

Split-screen

The split-screen overlay operates essentially the same as the others: add a clip by tapping the Split-Screen button. Initially the screen is split vertically. To control which clip appears in the frame, do the following:

1. Select the overlay.

2. In the Video controls that appear at the bottom of the screen, tap the Split-Screen button.

3. Choose how the split-screen appears: vertically or horizontally, with the option to swap the panes (3.24).

▶ **NOTE** Any overlay can be converted to a different type. If you think a split-screen would work better than a picture-in-picture effect, for example, select the overlay in the timeline and tap the Split-Screen button.

▶ **TIP** As you're working on editing your movie, you can tap the Undo button to reverse the last action. But what if you tap Undo a few too many times? Touch and hold the Undo button, which reveals a Redo option.

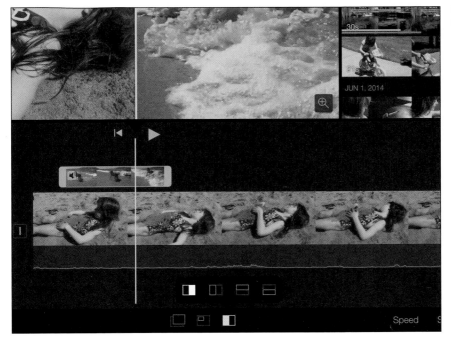

3.24 Editing a split-screen overlay

Remove an overlay

Just as you would remove a regular clip, drag an overlay out of the timeline to make it disappear in a puff of smoke. Or, select it and tap the trash button at the bottom of the screen.

Overlays are attached to the clips on which they sit, which means that moving or deleting the base clip also moves or deletes the overlay.

Change a Clip's Speed

As you know from Chapter 2, and particularly if you own an iPhone 5s, you can get dramatic results by slowing down playback. iMovie recognizes the iPhone 5s Slo-Mo mode, which gives you 120 frames per second to play with, but it can also slow down or speed up regular footage shot at other speeds. With a couple of taps, you can compress a sunset without actually shooting and assembling a genuine time-lapse video. And let's not forget the Benny Hill effect of speeding up people's ordinary movements.

To change the speed of a clip, do the following:

1. Select a clip in the timeline.

2. In the Video options that appear at the bottom of the screen, tap the Speed button.

3. Drag the Speed slider to the left to slow the clip down or to the right to speed it up (3.25).

A speed change is applied to the entire clip. If you want speed variations within a scene, split the clip and change the speed of individual sections.

▶ **TIP** Remember that when you change the clip's speed, you also change the speed of the audio. Unless you intend to make people sound like chipmunks, mute the speed-changed clip.

▶ **TIP** Slo-Mo clips shot on the iPhone 5s can be sped up only to 1x (normal speed).

▶ **TIP** When you add a Slo-Mo clip to the timeline, iMovie recognizes that it's 120 fps and plays the entire clip in slow motion. You can tell iMovie to ignore the slow-motion setting and play the clip at normal speed, if you prefer to adjust the speed yourself later. Go to Settings > iMovie and disable the Automatic Slow-Motion Effect option.

3.25 Speed control

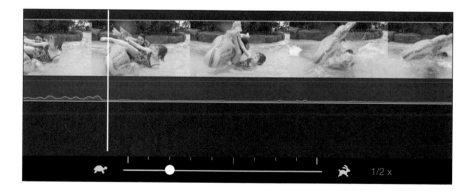

Create a Freeze Frame

Remember, the footage in the timeline is composed of hundreds or thousands of individual frames. When played in sequence they convey movement, but nothing says you can't stop time when it suits you. The Freeze feature pulls a frame out as a still image for the duration you want.

1. In the timeline, position the playhead over the frame you want to freeze.

2. Tap to select the clip.

3. From the Video options that appear at the bottom of the screen, tap the Freeze button. The clip is split and a new still image is added (3.26).

4. The freeze frame appears for 2 seconds when the movie is played. Drag the selection handles to increase or decrease the duration.

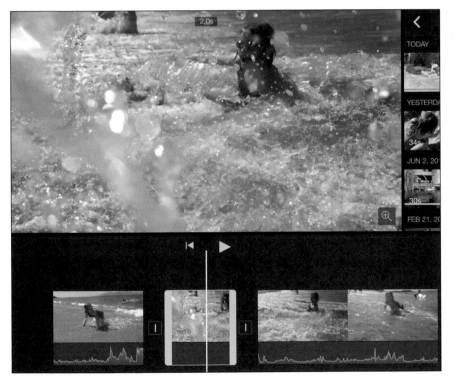

3.26 This freeze frame moment can't be wrong.

Edit Transitions

iMovie automatically adds a cross dissolve transition between every clip, whether you want it or not. That's not to enforce a transition style on your projects, but rather to have a transition icon you can touch and adjust easily.

Even when you want no transition at all, the icon stays put—notice the transitions that surround the freeze frame in the figure on the previous page. The playhead skips right over them without disrupting playback. You could change them to something like the Fade to White transition (and throw in a camera click sound) to simulate the effect of capturing a still photo.

1. Select a transition icon to reveal the Transition settings at the bottom of the screen (3.27).

2. Tap to choose the type of transition: None (creating an abrupt jump cut between the clips on either side), Theme, Cross Dissolve, Wipe, Push, or Fade to Black (or White).

   The appearance of the Theme transition depends on which theme you chose for your project. To change the theme, tap the Project Settings button and tap a new one, as described earlier in the chapter.

   When you tap the Wipe and Push transitions, choose a direction for the effect. The Fade to Black transition offers a Fade to White option.

3. Tap the duration in the Transition settings to choose an amount.

4. To apply the changes, tap outside the transition.

3.27 Choose a transition style and duration.

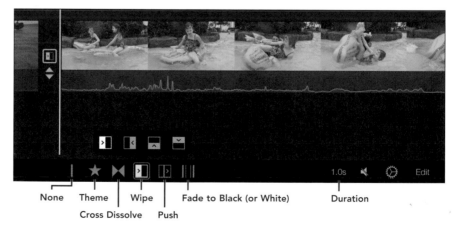

None   Theme   Wipe   Fade to Black (or White)   Duration
Cross Dissolve   Push

The important thing to know about transitions is how they affect the timing of the clips on either side of them. A straightforward cut, where the transition is set to None, jumps from one clip to the next. The other transitions, however, need to overlap footage to accomplish their effects.

For example, suppose you have a video that contains two 5-second clips. With the transition set to None, the movie's duration is 10 seconds (3.28).

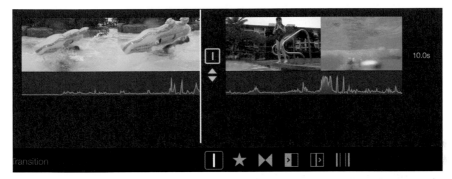

3.28 No transition

Now, let's change the transition to Cross Dissolve and give it a duration of 1 second. The length of the movie becomes 9 seconds, even though you didn't trim any of the footage, because iMovie needs to overlap the clips; the transition uses half a second from each (3.29).

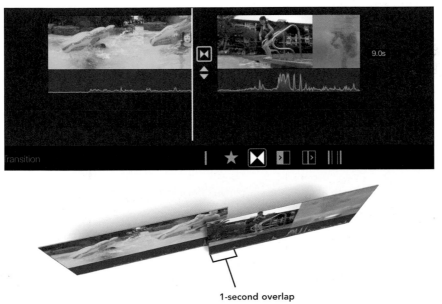

3.29 Cross Dissolve transition

1-second overlap

Apply a Fade In or Fade Out to the Movie

Instead of starting with the first frame of the first clip, you may want to begin your movie with a fade in from black. The Project Settings window includes single-switch options for adding fades to the start and end of a project.

1. Tap the Project Settings button (the gear) to open the Project Settings window.

2. Tap the switch next to "Fade in from black" or "Fade out to black" (or both) to change the setting from Off to On.

3. Tap outside the window to apply the setting.

Use the Precision Editor

It's important to understand the way transitions work to best take advantage of one of iMovie's most powerful features, the Precision Editor. It shows you all the footage around the edit, gives you a visual representation of what footage is being used in the transition, and makes it easier to choose the ending and starting frames of clips.

1. Tap a transition icon to select it, and then tap the double-triangle icon to display the Precision Editor (3.30). Or, pinch outward vertically on a transition.

2. Do any of the following to adjust the edit point:

   • Drag the transition itself to reposition the edit point without changing the duration of the surrounding clips.

   • Drag the top handle to change the end point of the previous clip without adjusting the next clip.

   • Drag the bottom handle to change the start point of the next clip without adjusting the previous clip.

3. Tap the triangle icons, or pinch two fingers together, to close the Precision Editor.

▶ **NOTE** It's possible to adjust the duration of the transition from within the Precision Editor. Tap the duration amount at the bottom of the screen.

Normal editing in the timeline

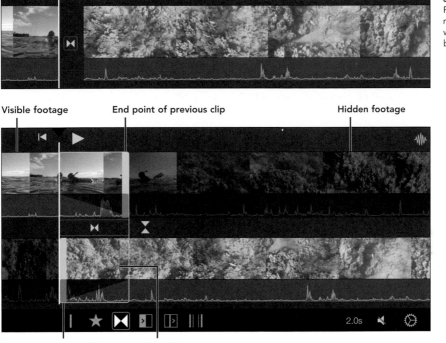

3.30 Use the Precision Editor to more accurately set where adjoining clips begin and end.

Visible footage   End point of previous clip   Hidden footage

Start point of next clip   Transition

2.0s

Add a Title

Every clip can have a title; in fact, you could say that every clip already has one, but it's hidden by default. iMovie offers several templates for titles, either based on the project theme or several preset effects.

1. Select a clip to view the Video settings at the bottom of the screen.

2. Tap the Title button; the default style is None.

3. Choose a title style: Opening, Middle, or Closing. The styles depend on the project's theme and are designed for common spots in your movie. For example, Opening is good for titles at the start of a movie and can occupy the entire screen, while Middle typically runs a title at the bottom of the screen without obscuring your video. Of course, you can choose whichever style you want at any point in your movie.

4. Tap the text field in the Viewer, and enter your title text (3.31).

5. Tap Done in the virtual keyboard to stop editing the title.

6. To apply one of the preset styles, tap the Title button that appears in the lower-right corner of the screen and choose a style (3.32). The styles can also appear in the center of the video or in the lower portion; specify which position by tapping Center or Lower at the bottom of the screen.

7. Tap outside the selected clip to apply the title.

3.31 Entering text in a theme title

3.32 Choosing a title style

Add a title to just a portion of a clip

A title spans the entire length of a clip—even if the clip is several minutes long. If you want the title to appear on just a portion, such as the first few seconds, do the following:

1. Position the playhead in the clip where you want the title to end.

2. Split the clip.

3. Select the portion you want, and add a title to it (3.33).

Title applied

3.33 Split a clip to display a title over just a portion of it.

Specify a Location

When you shoot video on the iPhone or iPad, the camera embeds location data in the photos and video they capture, thanks to their built-in assisted-GPS technologies. iMovie reads that data, too, and gives you the option of using it in titles and, creatively, a few themes.

1. Select a clip to view the Video settings at the bottom of the screen.

2. Tap the Title button and choose a title.

3. Tap the Location button (which looks like a pin).

4. If location information was saved with the clip, it appears in the Location window (3.34). To change the location, do one of the following:

   • To use your current location, tap the arrow button.

   • To find a location, tap the Search button to search iMovie's database of locations. Tap the closest match to use it.

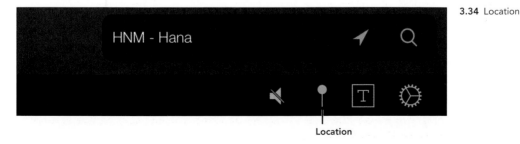

3.34 Location

Location

HNM - HANA

Wish you were here!

NO. 1032

Maui Vacation

5. You can also change the label to something more specific, like a neighborhood or restaurant name. Tap the label and enter new text; it won't change the underlying location data. For example, the Travel theme adds a location marker to a map in its Opening title; the marker stays in place, but its label changes.

6. Tap outside the clip to deselect it and exit the Title settings.

▶ **TIP** In most themes, the location appears as a subhead below the title. If you don't want to announce the location, why not put that text to good use? In the Location window, enter any text you wish to display, even if it has nothing to do with location (3.35).

3.35 Use the Location line as a subhead.

Maui Vacation
The Road to Hana

Add and Edit Photos

Still photos can be just as important as video in your movie, so iMovie imports photos to the timeline as well. They aren't static, either. The Ken Burns effect—where the "camera" appears to zoom and move over the image to give it motion—is applied to every photo (whether you want the effect or not).

▶ **NOTE** As with video, if you capture photos from within iMovie, those images are restricted to the project that was active when you did the shooting.

3.36 Photos in the Media Library

To add photos to your project, do the following:

1. Position the playhead in the timeline where you want a new photo to appear.

2. Go to the Media Library and tap the Photos button to view available photo albums.

3. Tap an album name to view its photos (3.36).

4. To preview a photo, touch and hold its thumbnail.

5. Tap the photo thumbnail once to add it to the timeline.

▶ **TIP** If iMovie detects faces in the photo, it will attempt to keep them within the frame.

Edit the Ken Burns Effect

The Ken Burns effect is based on the position of the frame at the beginning and end of the clip. iMovie determines how best to make the camera move from one state to the other.

1. In the timeline, tap a photo you've imported to select it.

2. Tap the Start button in the Viewer to move the playhead to the first frame of the clip, if it's not already positioned there (3.37).

3. Position the starting frame the way you wish: Pinch inward or outward to zoom in or out on the frame. Drag to position it in the frame.

3.37 Editing the Ken Burns effect

4. Tap the End button to move the playhead to the last frame of the clip.

5. Adjust the image to the way you want it to appear at the end of the sequence.

6. Deselect the clip. iMovie builds the animation between the Start and End frames automatically as the movie plays.

Disable the Ken Burns Effect

Unfortunately, there's no easy control to turn off the Ken Burns effect and just display a static photo. However, a(n imperfect) workaround is possible.

1. Tap the Start button.

2. Pinch the image onscreen so you can see all of its edges (zoomed out), and then release it—iMovie snaps it back into place with a minimal amount of zoom applied.

3. Tap the End button and repeat step 2 to let iMovie snap it into place.

4. Tap Done to stop editing the photo.

Change a Clip's Volume Level

Even when you do your best to record good audio, sometimes volume levels don't match up from clip to clip, or you just want to mute a clip.

1. Select a clip in the timeline to display the Clip settings.

2. Tap the Audio button.

3. Drag the volume slider to increase or decrease the overall level (3.38). To mute, tap the speaker icon, which sets the audio to zero.

▶ **NOTE** Whenever a video clip with audio appears over a background song, the song is automatically ducked (made softer). Unfortunately, iMovie offers no controls for specifying the amount of ducking to apply.

Audio Waveforms button

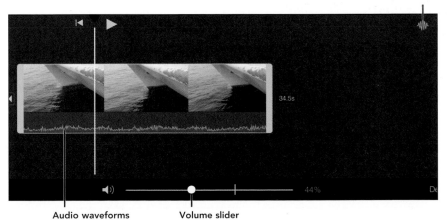

3.38 Change a clip's volume in the Clip Settings window.

Audio waveforms   Volume slider

Detach an Audio Clip

In most cases, video clips arrive with sound attached, so iMovie treats the video and audio as a single clip to simplify things. That embedded audio really is a separate element, though. Sometimes it's helpful to detach it and work with it as a separate clip, such as when you want to fade the audio or change the volume of specific areas.

1. Select the video clip you want to edit.

2. In the Clip tools at the bottom of the screen, tap Audio.

3. Tap the Detach button. A new audio clip appears below the video clip (3.39). Note that the audio also includes the portion used in the transition.

3.39 Detached audio

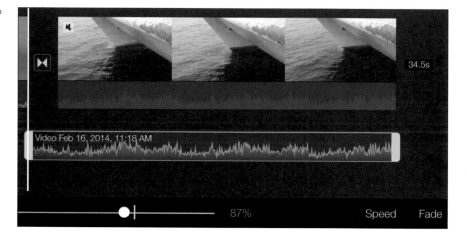

To be more accurate, the detached audio is actually a new *copy* of the audio—the waveforms in the video clip are still present, but the clip is automatically muted when detaching audio. So, if you change your mind or edit the detached audio clip beyond recognition, you can always delete it and re-detach the original audio.

▶ **NOTE** Even though the audio is detached, it's still connected to the source video clip. Moving the video clip to a new location on the timeline also moves the detached audio, too.

Fade an Audio Clip

When a video clip ends at an abrupt cut and changes to the next clip, we think nothing of it. We're so accustomed to jump cuts that our brains provide the missing context needed to make sense of what we're seeing. If I show a clip of a man, then cut to a clip of a mountain, you won't get confused thinking the man had turned into a mountain; you assume the mountain must be nearby or establishes the location of the next scene.

Audio, however, is a different matter. An abrupt audio cut can be jarring and draws attention to itself. To compensate, editors fade the volume in or out, changing the audio gradually, even in a short timeframe. Transitions automatically fade the audio, as does choosing to fade the movie in or out from black (in the project settings).

1. Detach a video clip's audio as described on the opposite page.

2. Tap the Fade button in the Clip tools.

3. Drag the Fade controls (the yellow triangles) to set the duration of the fade (3.40). A faint ramp within the clip indicates the fade.

4. Tap outside the clip to deselect it, or tap the Trim button to go back to the trimming mode.

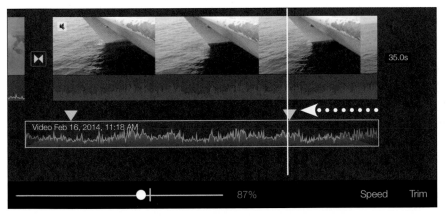

3.40 Fading the audio clip

Split an Audio Clip

Once detached, an audio clip can be edited using the same basic techniques as editing a video clip. Trim the edges to change the duration, duplicate the clip, or split it. What's not currently possible, alas, is to adjust the volume level within a clip; the volume applies to the entire clip.

To work around this limitation, split the audio into discrete sections and change their volume levels. For example, if the audio spikes at some point—someone coughs, a loud noise occurs near the microphone, or the volume of the scene fluctuates wildly—you can isolate that section and drop the level. It's not a perfect solution, but it's a workable one.

1. Detach the audio clip, if you haven't already done so.

2. Position the playhead at the start of the section you want to change.

3. Select the audio clip.

4. From the Clip tools, tap the ellipses button and choose Split. Or, swipe from top to bottom at the playhead.

5. Split the remaining portion of the clip to isolate (3.41).

   ▶ **TIP** It helps to see more detail when editing audio clips. Pinch outward horizontally to stretch the timeline.

3.41 Splitting an audio clip

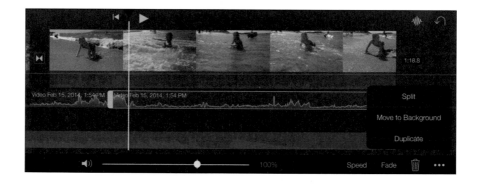

6. Select the isolated section.

7. Adjust the volume slider to the level you want; notice that the waveform lowers to reflect the change (3.42).

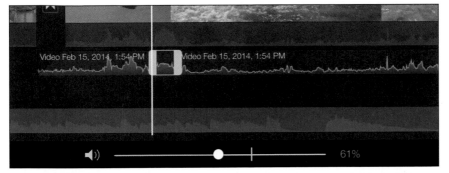

► **TIP** Even after you split a detached audio clip, the sections remain together
with the parent video clip if you move the video to another section of the
timeline.

Add Background Music

In iMovie, some audio clips are treated differently than others. A special
background music track loops behind the video, and always starts at the
beginning of the movie; it can't be pinned to a specific location in the
movie. This is the type of track that's used when you opt to include the
music included with a project theme. You can also add your own audio
tracks as foreground audio clips, but the background music track is a good
place to start. Only one background song is allowed at a time.

Add automatic theme music

1. Tap the Project Settings button.

2. Tap the Theme Music switch so it's set to On.

3. Tap outside the Project Settings window to apply the setting.

Add a background music clip

1. Go to the Media Library and tap the Audio button.

2. Choose an audio source (**3.43, on the next page**). In addition to iMovie's
   theme music selections, the Audio window gives you access to your
   iTunes music library, sorted by playlists, albums, artists, or songs. If
   you've added audio from another source, such as a GarageBand song,
   you'll also see an Imported option.

3.43 Audio window

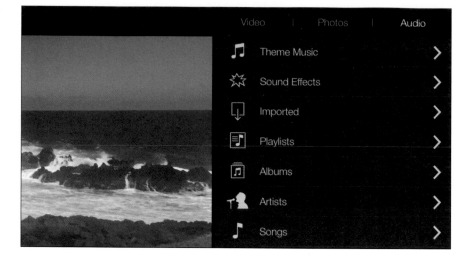

3. Tap the name of a song to select it.

4. Tap the Play button that appears to preview the song, or tap the Add button to include it in your project. It appears as a green track under the video clips in the timeline (3.44).

3.44 A background song added to the timeline

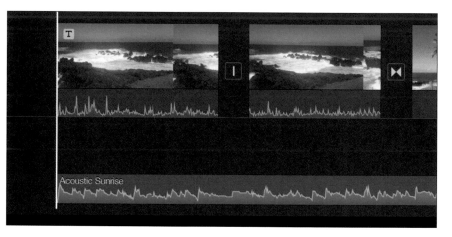

▶ **NOTE** iMovie does not import any music encumbered with Apple's Fair-Play DRM scheme; those tracks appear in the song list, but in gray. Apple abandoned DRM for music tracks a while ago, but you may still have tracks in your iTunes library from before the switch. Apple's iTunes Match service (which costs $24.99 a year) enables you to re-download non-DRM versions of your music (which are often better-quality copies at higher bit rates). If you do subscribe to iTunes Match, your music is synced via iCloud instead of through iTunes on your computer, so you'll need to download any songs you wish to use in your projects from within the Music app; songs only on iCloud also appear in gray text with "(Unavailable)" appended to the titles.

Aside from the fact that a background song can't be repositioned in the timeline, you can edit it like most clips. Tap to select it, and then adjust its duration using the selection handles; then adjust the clip's overall volume. To fade the audio at the start or end, tap the Fade button and drag the fade marker that appears (3.45).

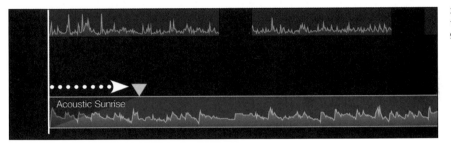

3.45 Applying a fade to the background song

> ▶ **TIP** Music written for each theme is available to add to any project, not just to movies with those themes. In the Audio window, tap Theme Music and choose any song you wish.

Add Foreground Audio

Any audio that's not a background song or embedded in a video clip is treated as *foreground audio*, including other music from the Music app, sound effects, and voiceovers. Up to three foreground tracks can appear on the timeline.

1. Position the playhead at the section where you want the clip to start.

2. In the Media Library, tap the Audio button.

3. Tap the Sound Effects button to view a list of available effects, or browse your music library (but see the item on the next page regading clip length).

4. Tap the name of the clip you want to use.

5. Tap the Play button to preview the audio, or tap the Add button to put it on the timeline (3.46).

3.46 Sound effects appear on tracks below the video but above the back-ground song.

Move audio clips between foreground and background

How does iMovie tell the difference between a foreground audio clip and a background audio clip? It assumes any clip longer than 1 minute is a back-ground song; anything shorter is foreground audio. However, you can move tracks between the background and the foreground.

1. Select an audio track you want to move.

2. Tap the ellipses (…) button.

3. Choose Move to Foreground or Move to Background.

Add a Voiceover

Most of the time, your videos can speak for themselves. On occasion, though, you may want to provide narration or a commentary track that plays over the footage. iMovie's audio import feature lets you record your voice (or any sound, for that matter) into the timeline.

1. Position the playhead in your movie where you want to begin record-ing audio.

2. Tap the Record button (the microphone at the bottom of the screen) to bring up the Ready to Record window.

3. When you're ready to start capturing audio, tap the Record button in the window. iMovie counts down from 3 to 1 and begins recording (3.47).

4. Tap the Stop button to end recording. The recorded clip appears as a purple audio clip below the video in the timeline.

5. Choose what to do with the recorded clip: Tap Review to listen to it; tap Retake to record again; tap Cancel to delete the recording; or tap Accept to keep it in your project (3.48).

Feel free to record multiple takes, but keep in mind that you can have only three audio tracks in one spot at a time. Also, mute the other takes before you record a new one.

3.47 Recording a voiceover

3.48 Reviewing the voiceover

Add Just Audio from a Video Clip

Remember the advice in Chapter 2 about shooting B-roll footage to make sure you have plenty of interesting coverage for your movie? That advice also applies to shooting to capture the audio from a scene. For example, you may want a consistent sound of the surf at a beach to appear behind several video clips, each of which may have slightly different sounds. Or maybe you want the audio of an interview, but for the visual you prefer to include only photos. In these situations, you can import just the audio from a video clip.

1. Position the playhead where you want the audio to begin.

2. In the Media Library, tap the Video button to locate the clip you wish to import.

3. Tap to select the clip, and optionally trim it if needed.

4. Tap the ellipses button to reveal the additional import options (3.49).

5. Tap the Add Audio Only button to add the audio portion to the movie. It appears as a dark blue foreground track (3.50).

3.49 Add only the audio from a video track.

Add Audio Only

3.50 The audio track on the timeline

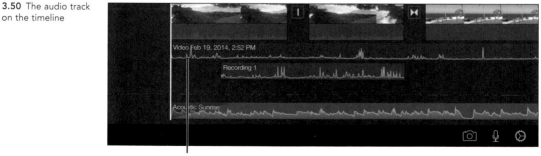

Track added

Pinnacle Studio

iMovie for iOS is a deliberate re-envisioning of how to edit video on a touch-based interface, and is quite different from the way much editing software works. If you learned how to edit video before, say, six or seven years ago, iMovie probably feels a bit alien. For an interface that's more "traditional" (if you can even use that term with the ever-changing field of technology), Pinnacle Studio for iPad offers a workflow and interface that are more comfortable for some people (**3.51**).

For example, to add a transition, you drag it into place from the library of transitions; similarly, drag titles on top of clips in the timeline. Pinnacle Studio also includes features you won't find in iMovie. I like that it has a separate Storyboard track to view your clips independently of their lengths, and you have more control over where titles appear onscreen. It's also easy to replace a clip on the timeline without disrupting the movie's timing: Drag a clip from the library onto a storyboard clip.

However, the app also brings back an annoyance that iMovie leaves behind: the need to render titles and some effects before the video plays back smoothly. That irritation, however, may be worth it if Pinnacle's way of working suits you better.

3.51 Pinnacle Studio

CHAPTER 4

Compose a Soundtrack in GarageBand

You don't have to be a musician to create music for your movies. Using Apple's GarageBand app on the iPhone or iPad, you can easily assemble a song or specific musical cues out of pre-recorded loops.

If the included loops don't cut it, GarageBand also includes a bunch of Smart Instruments that let you play preset grooves or individual notes that seamlessly conform to the song's tempo and key.

If you are a musician, even better! Connect an instrument—like a guitar or a MIDI keyboard—or a microphone to the iOS device and record your own compositions. GarageBand Includes guitar amp simulations that can make you and your electric guitar sound like anything from a surf-rocker to a hair-metal god. It also has vocal effects that can give a professional polish to your voice or make you sound like a monster or a robot. And for you keyboard play-ers, the included piano, synthesizer, and string sounds will add lush beauty or a techno edge to your movie soundtrack.

Open the Garage(Band)

Don't be intimidated if you can't even fumble through "Chopsticks." GarageBand has a few tricks up its sleeve even for the musically inept.

The app is built around what Apple calls Touch Instruments. These are instruments you can play directly on the iPad or iPhone, and they're a natural for the Multi-Touch interface. You need to open one of the instruments in order to get to the included loops, so let's start there.

Open GarageBand. If this is your first time in the app, it will open to the Touch Instrument browser (4.1). Choose Keyboard.

4.1 Instruments at your fingertips

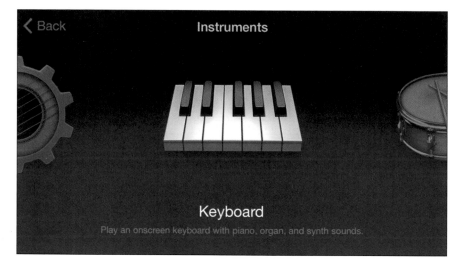

> ▶ **NOTE** If you've played with GarageBand before, you may wind up on a different screen. If you see a group of song previews, possibly with names like "My Song" and "My Song 2," tap the + in the upper-left corner of the screen to create a new song and open the Touch Instrument browser. In most other screens, tap the word Instruments in the upper-left corner to open the browser.

Test-Drive the Touch Instruments

Allow me a moment to extol the virtues of GarageBand before we jump into building a song out of loops. If the app were just an instrument synthesizer, that would be fine. But you'll find that GarageBand is a remarkably deep program. Yes, you can play a keyboard that sounds like a grand piano, but there are also modes that help you avoid making it sound like you've never touched an instrument in your life (even if that's true). For example, you can switch to different scales that eliminate the "bad" notes and leave you with only the notes of that particular scale. This makes it impossible to play a wrong note!

1. Tap the Scale button to the right of the screen, above the keyboard. It shows two musical notes. On the iPad, it conveniently says "Scale."

2. Choose Major Blues from the list of options (**4.2**).

3. The keyboard changes from the usual collection of black and white keys to a set of all white keys with periodic gray keys labelled C3, C4, and so on. Slide your finger back and forth along the keyboard and the piano plays a jazzy scale that sounds like a smoky St. Louis bar in the 1930s.

4. Tap the Grand Piano icon in the top half of the screen to change to a different keyboard instrument; on the iPhone, tap the triangle in the upper left and then tap Grand Piano. In addition to pianos, you'll find two electric pianos, a few organs, and a bunch of synthesizers. To find the synths, tap one of the category tabs (such as Classics or Bass). Each reveals a different species of synth sound. Try out a few and see what they each sound like.

Some of the synth sounds have a Pitch option enabled that lets you slide your finger across the keyboard to bend from note to note. Spectrum Echo, under the Classics tab, is a great example.

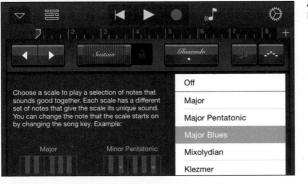

4.2 Choosing a keyboard scale

Calculate Tempo from Movie Length

While working in iMovie, you'll no doubt encounter a situation where you need a piece of music to fill a specific chunk of time. While GarageBand on the Mac lets you change the ruler to show minutes and seconds, the iOS version does not. There are ways around this restriction, though, if you're willing to do a few easy calculations.

If you know you have, say, 8 seconds of video to fill, and you need to create a piece of music to fit, the trick is figuring out how many measures and what tempo your song needs to be. Fortunately, an app called Audiofile Calc can calculate this for you. The app conveniently includes a song length calculator (4.3). In most cases, you need to use a little trial and error to get a workable solution, since the length is a product of the equation and not a variable you can enter yourself.

4.3 Audiofile Calc

The vast majority of songs (and almost all the Apple Loops in GarageBand) are four beats per bar, so you can usually leave the last field set to 4.

Working backwards, the number of bars refers to the length of your piece in musical "measures." A measure is a segment of musical time defined by the number of beats per bar, set in the bottom field. Each measure, or each count of "1-2-3-4," helps define the musical pulse of a song and the pattern of strong and weak beats that give a song its rhythm. Most Western music is broken up into subsections of four, eight, or sixteen measures, so sticking with multiples of four is a good idea unless you have a good reason to do otherwise.

The Tempo field determines how fast your piece is. Anything below 70 or 80 beats per minute (BPM) is considered slow, 80–112 BPM is a medium tempo, and 112–140 BPM is fast. Anything above 140 BPM or so is quite fast, and 180 BPM and above is extremely fast. If you haven't already worked out a rough tempo in GarageBand, it may be useful to play with some options and see what feels right for your movie. Tempo is an important consideration and has a huge impact on the emotional impact of the music.

Once you've entered all the required information, Audiofile Calc gives you the resulting length. Adjust the Tempo and Bars fields until you arrive at your video length, then input the resulting information into GarageBand.

Open the Settings menu (on the iPad, tap the wrench icon; on the iPhone, tap the gear and then choose Song), and tap the Tempo button (4.4). Listen to how it works musically. You may find that the tempo is too fast or that the number of bars doesn't feel right and you need to adjust accordingly.

▶ **TIP** It's not difficult to calculate the exact BPM yourself using a simple math formula: BPM = Number of Measures x 240 / Length in Seconds. 240 is the number of beats per measure (4) times 60 (seconds in a minute), and dividing that by the ultimate length of the piece gives you the number of beats per minute of your GarageBand song. Easy!

4.4 Changing tempo

Build a Soundtrack Using Loops

Okay, it's time to build a soundtrack for your video. In addition to playable instruments, GarageBand includes a number of pre-recorded loops that make it easy to build a song from scratch. The trick is, the Loop browser is a bit harder to find on the iPad and iPhone version of GarageBand than it is on the Mac. It also has fewer loops available, but there are still plenty to get you started.

Create a New Song

When you opened the Keyboard instrument earlier, GarageBand automatically created a new song using that instrument. Since you're building a brand new song, you want to make sure you begin with an empty canvas.

1. In the upper-left corner of the Keyboard window, tap My Songs; on the iPhone, tap the disclosure triangle to reveal My Songs. GarageBand automatically saves your current creation as "My Song," but that's okay. You can delete it later if you like.

2. Tap the + icon in the upper-left corner to create a new, empty song and reopen the Touch Instrument browser (4.5). Since you're going to be working with loops, it doesn't really matter which instrument you choose.

3. Tap Keyboard again to open the Keyboard instrument.

4.5 Create a new song.

Browse Through the Loops

Since the Loop browser isn't available from any of the Instrument screens, switch to Tracks view by tapping the Tracks view button in the control bar across the top of the screen. Tracks view shows your song as a timeline, much like iMovie displays your movie. The left side of the screen is the beginning of your song, and the instruments stack from top to bottom.

On the iPhone, Tracks view isn't visible in a new song until you record something. Tap the Record button, play a few notes, and tap Play again to stop recording. Now the View button should be visible on the left side of the control bar.

At first, you see a fairly empty screen, with a timeline across the top and a small piano icon in the upper-left corner. In the control bar, tap the Loop browser button (4.6). The Loop browser contains several hundred Apple Loops in a wide variety of musical genres, from rock and electronic to orchestral and world music. These can be great starting points for your own compositions or can even form complete soundtracks in their own right. Tap a few of the loop names to hear what they sound like.

▶ **TIP** Use the volume slider at the bottom of the Loop browser to audition loops at a louder or softer volume (4.7).

Tracks view button   Loop browser

4.6 Browsing loops

4.7 Preview volume

Add Loops to Your Song

As you're about to see, building a song from loops is a fast and easy way to create a simple soundtrack for your video. You don't need any musical skill, and there are no rules to follow. The only requirement is that you end up with something that you like and that works with your video project. I'm going to build a song using specific loops by way of example, but of course you can use whichever loops you want.

1. In the Loop browser, scroll through the list until you get to Cheerful Mandolin 10. Tap the name to preview it. Tap the loop again to stop playback.

2. Drag the loop below the piano track in the timeline (4.8). Align the left edge of the loop—which at this point looks like an empty blue rectangle—with the left edge of the timeline, so it starts at 1 on the ruler.

3. Tap the Play button at the top of the screen to hear your song so far.

    If you hear a tick-tock sound as your mandolin is playing, that's the metronome. It's turned on by default to make it easier to play Touch Instruments in time with the beat. Since you're using loops, which are automatically in time, turn off the metronome by tapping the Settings button in the upper-right corner and turning the Metronome switch off. Now you should only hear the mandolin.

4.8 Adding a loop

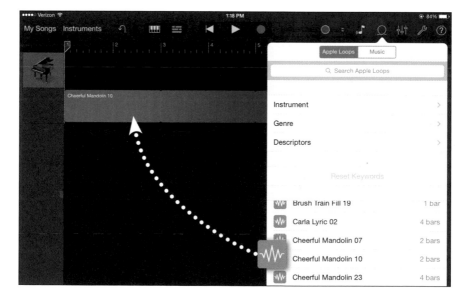

Before you add another track to the piece, it might look nicer if you delete the empty piano track at the top of the timeline. Tap the piano icon in the track header, then tap it again. Tap Delete to remove the track (4.9).

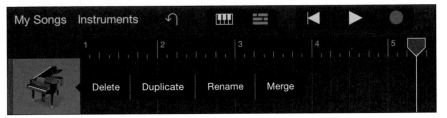

4.9 Removing the piano track

Build the Soundtrack

The mandolin is a great start, but it's a little boring on its own. It would sound better if it had some company. Drums could add some energy. Let's find a good drum beat to add to the song.

1. Tap Play in the control bar to hear your song, which continues to play until you tap Stop. This lets you audition new loops in context with the mandolin part.

2. Open the Loop browser.

3. Since there are hundreds of loops in the list, it can be helpful to narrow down your selection to make it easier to find what you're looking for. At the top of the Loop browser, tap Instrument, then tap Kits to hide all the loops except drum kits.

4. Tap Crowd Groove Drumset 06 to hear it alongside the mandolin.

5. Drag it to the timeline under the mandolin. Remember to align the beginning of the loop with the 1 on the ruler (4.10).

4.10 Second loop added

6. With the song still playing, tap the Loop browser again.

7. Tap Instrument at the top of the browser, then tap Tambourine.

8. Drag Tambourine 02 to the timeline under the drum track.

▶ **TIP** If you need more precision while editing, zoom in on the timeline by pinching out with your fingers from anywhere in the arrange area.

▶ **TIP** While many Apple Loops sound great together, not all of them will work in every context. If you come across two loops that sound awful together, don't panic. This is the nature of making music with loops. You never know if two loops will work together until you try them, and sometimes a combination that makes no sense on paper will end up being the best part of your song.

Change the Duration of a Loop

In some cases, you may not want a loop to continue through the entire section. To shorten a loop, tap to select it; a tiny circular arrow appears on the right handle. Drag the handle to the left to shorten it (4.11).

4.11 Shortening the loop length

Change the Volume of a Track

The piece is getting more interesting, but it still needs more. One of my favorite techniques when writing soundtracks is to mix instruments that don't technically belong together. So far, you've got a fairly mellow acoustic song. What would happen if you added a distorted guitar? Open the Loop browser again, narrow your selection to Guitars, and drag Classic Attitude Rock 18 to the beginning of the song.

When you play back your piece now, the electric guitar dominates the other instruments and sounds far too loud. Wouldn't it be great if there were a way to turn it down without affecting the volume of the other instruments? This is where having each instrument on its own track becomes helpful.

If one instrument is too loud or too quiet, you can adjust the volume of that one instrument while keeping the others at their original levels.

Drag one of the track icons to the right to reveal the track controls (4.12).

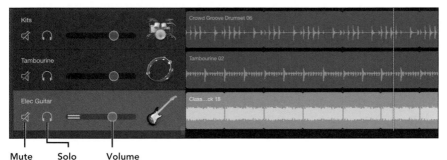

4.12 Track volume controls

Mute   Solo   Volume

In addition to the instrument name, the track controls feature a Mute button, which mutes the track, a Solo button, which mutes all the other tracks and allows you to hear one track in isolation, and a volume slider, which adjusts the volume of the track.

Turn down the Electric Guitar track by dragging the volume slider to the left until it sits nicely in the background. While you're at it, adjust the volume of other tracks if you wish. I turned down the tambourine a little as well.

▶ **TIP** To hear your song with and without the electric guitar, tap the Mute button on the guitar track. That silences the guitar and grays out the region to make it easy to see which tracks are muted (4.13). Un-mute the track to hear the energy and bite the guitar adds to the song.

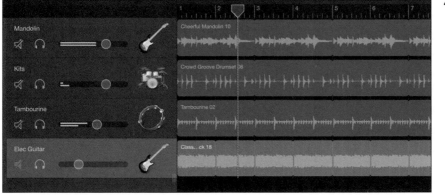

4.13 Track muted

Add a Bassline

To finish the song, it might be good to have a bass for some low-frequency grounding. Instead of adding a loop this time, you're going to experiment with Smart Instruments. Smart Instruments are a bit like loops, but they give you a lot more flexibility to add your own spin to a track. They're perfect for non-musicians who don't know how to play a particular instrument but still want the chance to be creative and do something a bit more personal than just adding loops to a song.

1. Tap Instruments in the control bar. Scroll through the Smart Instruments until you find Smart Bass, and tap the icon to open the instrument.

2. Tap the Liverpool icon in the upper-left corner of the screen and select the Picked bass (4.14).

4.14 Smart Bass

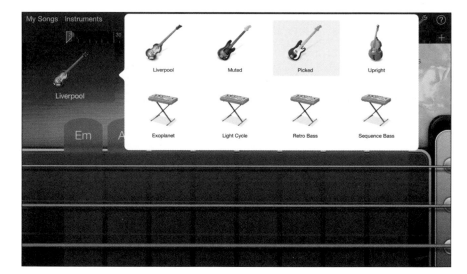

Notice that instead of a normal bass guitar neck, the Smart Bass displays four strings intersected by vertical gray stripes. Each of these stripes is labeled with the name of a chord in the key of your song.

Smart Instruments have several playback options including an Autoplay mode, which plays back pre-recorded sequences of notes in whatever chord you choose. This makes them act a bit like loops but with a lot more flexibility.

▶ **NOTE** By default, new GarageBand songs open in the key of C, which uses all the white keys on a piano. The "C" stripe on the Smart Bass instrument represents the C chord, which is the root, or "home," key in C. The other chords are all in the key of C as well, meaning that whatever chord you choose will sound harmonious.

3. Tap the 1 on the Autoplay knob (4.15). The strings disappear from the fretboard.

4. Tap the C chord and listen to the fancy groove.

   To record the bassline and add it to the song, you have to do something a little different than you did when adding loops. You need to actually record the bass to add it to the song.

5. Tap the Go to Beginning button in the control bar to make sure you start recording from the start of the song.

6. Tap the Record button and then quickly tap the C chord on the bass. You should hear the metronome count in for four beats and then hear the song start playing with the new Smart bassline.

   Once the recording reaches the end of the eight-bar section, playback loops back to the beginning of the song and GarageBand stops recording the bass and switches to playback mode.

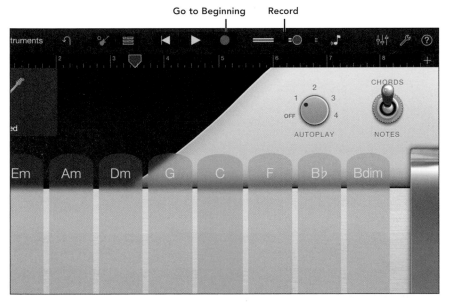

4.15 Autoplay engaged

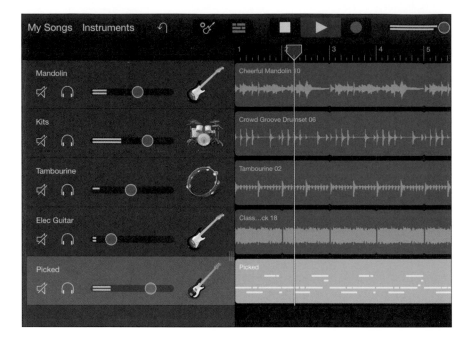

4.16 Smart Bass track added to the song

7. Switch back to Tracks view to see the new track in place (**4.16**).

▶   **TIP** The current song sounds good with the bass playing just one chord, but the idea behind Smart Instruments is that you can tap a new chord every measure or two to build a harmonic framework to your song. If you choose to play more with Smart Instruments, make sure you tap each chord a little early to give GarageBand a chance to change chords before the start of the new measure.

▶   **NOTE** Notice that the new bass track is green instead of blue like the other tracks. That's because it's what Apple calls a Software Instrument. The blue tracks are actual recordings of mandolins, drums, and tambourines—audio files that can't be modified aside from changing their volume. Green Software Instrument regions, on the other hand, are made up of individual notes that GarageBand plays back in real time. This means you can edit the notes in these regions if you want to change the part that a Smart Instrument played.

Extend Your Song Using Sections

Often, you'll want your song to be longer than the default eight measures. GarageBand organizes songs into sections like intro, verse, and chorus. Song Sections in GarageBand allow you to duplicate, lengthen, repeat, and move sections as you work to make writing and arranging your song easier.

You can access the Song Sections menu by tapping the Song Section button on the right side of the ruler. If you've been following along, your song currently contains only one eight-bar section. From the Song Section menu, you have several options:

- You can extend the current section by tapping the arrow to the right of Section A. The Automatic option is available for the last section in a song. It allows you to improvise as you record and lets GarageBand adjust the length of the new section to match your playing. With Automatic disabled, tap or swipe the number in the Manual field to shorten or lengthen the current section (**4.17**).

- Duplicate creates a copy of the current section and adds it to the end of the piece. This is handy if you want to create a variation of an existing section and don't want to redo all your hard work. To adjust the length of the new section, tap the Info button next to the section length.

- Add creates a new, blank section at the end of the song. Again, tapping the Info button allows you to alter the length of the new section.

- Once you have created new sections, tapping Edit lets you delete or rearrange them.

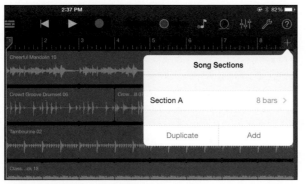

4.17 Extending the section

Add Loops to Existing Tracks

Now that all the tracks are in place, the song is beginning to sound a bit repetitive. It might be appropriate to add a drum fill or two to break up the monotony. Fortunately, GarageBand comes with drum loops specifically recorded for this purpose. Scroll through the Loop browser and notice the names of the two loops directly after Crowd Groove Drumset 06. Crowd Groove Fill 04 and Crowd Groove Fill 07 sound like they'll work perfectly.

Adding these loops to the existing drum track is extremely easy. Just as you did with the other loops, simply drag the loop from the browser into the timeline, only this time, drag it *on top* of the existing drum loop. Garage-Band intelligently makes room for the new loop, and even continues the existing drum loop after the fill. Add Crowd Groove Fill 07 at measure 4 on the ruler, and Crowd Groove Fill 04 at measure 8 (4.18). If you need help lining up the loops as you drag them, remember to use the yellow line marking the beginning of the loop. Line it up with the 4 and the 8 on the ruler and the fills will be in perfect sync.

4.18 Fill added to the drum kit

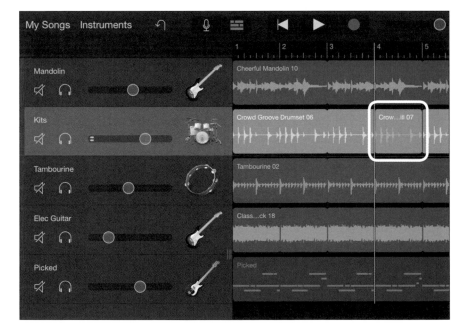

▶ **TIP** Much of Western music is written in phrases of four, eight, or sixteen bars. In pop music, ornamentation like drum and guitar fills are often used at the end of these phrases to add excitement and anticipation and to lead the listener into the next section.

Change Loop Duration

Sometimes, an Apple Loop you add to your song isn't the correct length. Perhaps you only want to use the first half of the loop and have that repeat. Or maybe you recorded a Smart Instrument track and want to loop only a portion of it. In these cases, you can edit the length of your region to customize the part.

In the case of Apple Loops that are already looping two or more times, tap the region to select it, then tap it again. Select Trim from the options that appear to select the original region and exclude the portion that's looping. Drag the end of the selected region to shorten it (4.19).

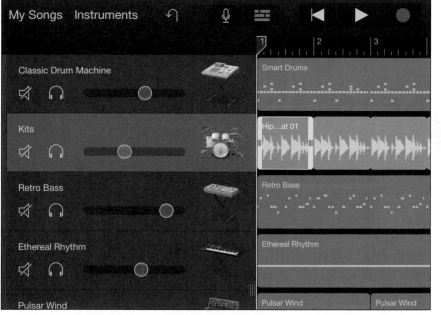

4.19 Changing loop duration

Rearrange Regions

In certain cases, you may want to rearrange the regions in your song—perhaps an active section needs to appear one measure earlier. When dealing with a track that's already full, this requires a bit of fancy maneuvering, but it's easy once you know the technique. If you just drag one region to a new spot on top of another, that deletes the second region. Instead, copy that region first.

This techniques works for regions that are separate (not looped copies of the same region).

1. Tap the region you want to move once to select it, tap it again, and choose Cut (4.20).

2. Drag the other region into the now vacant section.

3. Now drag the playhead to the beginning of the new opening, tap the vacant area in the track, and select Paste. Voilà! Regions swapped.

4.20 Rearrange regions.

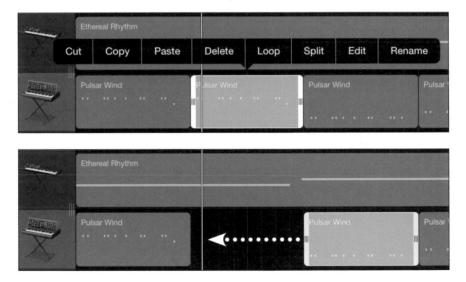

If you instead need to rearrange parts of a longer contiguous region, you need to split the region into pieces. Tap the region to select it, and tap it again to bring up the editing menu. Select Split, and drag the Split marker to the point where you want to split the regions (4.21). Drag the Split marker down to make the cut. You can continue to move the Split marker and make additional cuts as long as they're in the same region. To split a different region, select the region and choose Split again. Finally, to rearrange the resulting regions, follow the steps on the previous page.

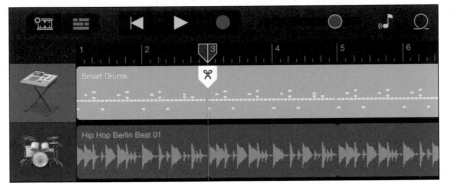

4.21 Splitting a region

Mix the Song

Listen to the song a few times and use the volume sliders to adjust the levels of the various tracks until they sound good together. When you feel good about the final mix, tap My Songs to save your creation. In the My Songs browser, tap the name of your new song to rename it (4.22). It's a good idea to rename songs you like, otherwise you may end up with "My Song 1" through "My Song 418" and it will become very difficult to locate a particular piece. If you recorded a song for a specific movie, it makes sense to put the movie name in the song title.

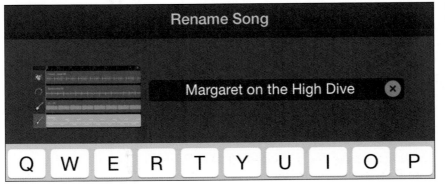

4.22 Give the piece a name.

Record Your Own Material

If you happen to sing or play a musical instrument, GarageBand becomes an even more powerful tool. Not only can you build a song from loops and Smart Instruments, you can also record your own performance. In some cases, this requires an extra piece of gear or two, but many of these accessories are quite affordable, and should be within the range of even modest budgets.

Record Acoustic Instruments

If you sing or play piano, acoustic guitar, violin, or any other acoustic instrument, adding yourself to a recording isn't difficult. You can either use the built-in mic on the iPad or iPhone or purchase a better-sounding option that connects to your device. Numerous options are available, from small mics that plug into the headphone jack to larger, more professional options that connect to the dock. In general with audio gear, the more you spend the better quality you get, so don't expect a professional-sounding recording from a $10 microphone. But with some care you can achieve excellent recordings with mics costing $150 or less.

▶ **TIP** Before you make a purchase, think about what options you want from a microphone. In many cases, acoustic instruments sound better recorded in stereo—guitars and pianos in particular. If you'd like the option of recording in stereo, make sure the mic you choose offers that option. If you're mostly going to be recording yourself singing or speaking, a mono microphone may be all you need.

Once you have a microphone, recording an acoustic instrument is a fairly easy process.

1. Find a good spot to record in. Generally speaking, you want a quiet location with good acoustics. Recordings of acoustic instruments always include at least some of the sound of the room. If you like the sound of your guitar in your living room, record yourself there. If it sounds even better in the closet, try that. The one thing you don't want to do is plop yourself somewhere without any consideration of how the environment sounds.

2. Connect your mic or use the built-in microphone. If you do use the built-in mic, know that the recording quality will not be as high as it would be with an external microphone.

3. Tap Instruments and select the Audio Recorder.

   The Audio Recorder is the simplest instrument in GarageBand. It has no controls, and the interface consists entirely of a large VU (volume unit) meter measuring the level of the incoming sound (4.23).

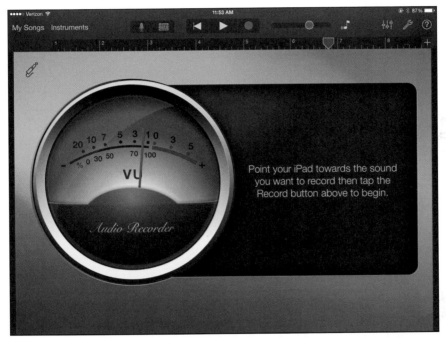

4.23 Recording audio through a microphone

4. Play or sing at the same volume you will be recording. Watch the VU meter. If it peaks into the red, turn down the input on the microphone (if possible), play or sing more quietly, or move the mic farther away.

5. If this is the first instrument in a new song, you may want to turn on the metronome to make it easier to sync other instruments with your playing. Tap the Song Settings button and turn on the metronome. You can also enable Count In if you want the metronome to tap for one measure before recording begins. This helps you internalize the tempo and lets you know when to start playing.

► **TIP** Headphones are useful when you need to hear the metronome or the other tracks in your song (an argument against a mic that uses the headphone jack). Otherwise, the recording will pick up the sound of the metronome.

6. When you're ready to record, tap the Go to Beginning button to move the playhead to the start of the section.

7. Tap Record and start playing or singing. Tap Stop when you're done.

Carefully listen to the recorded take with headphones or speakers, and make sure the recording sounds the way you want it to. If you made a mistake, re-record the section. If the sound quality is poor, try to assess what went wrong:

- **Is the recording too loud?** If so, it will likely sound distorted and look like a block of sound rather than distinct waveforms (4.24). Turn down the mic or move it farther from the source, and re-record your part.

4.24 Loud like golf pants

- **Is the recording too quiet?** In this case, turn up the mic, play or sing louder, or move the mic closer to the source.

- **Is the sound echoey or boomy?** You may be recording in too "live" a room. Large rooms with hard surfaces often sound quite reverberant and may not be right for certain instruments. Try moving to a different location.

- **Is the sound quality poor?** If you're using the built-in mic or a cheap external option, you may need a better alternative. Try moving the mic to a different location relative to the instrument. Sometimes even an inch or two can make a huge difference.

▶ **TIP** To add preset effects to your voice or recorded instrument, double-tap its track header. This opens up the previously viewed Audio Recorder, but now with eight effect options to choose from. Small Room and Large Room sound great on vocals, and Telephone is a favorite of mine on drum loops. If you're looking for additional effects, see "Going Further with GarageBand" to learn how to export your project to GarageBand for Mac.

▶ **NOTE** If you want to get really wacky, try out the Sampler instrument. It lets you record any sound you want and play it back on a musical keyboard. You can record yourself sneezing or your cat meowing and play it back melodically. It's a great, fun way to make almost any sound musical.

Connect an Electric Guitar or Bass

If you're the axe-wielding type, it's also a snap to use GarageBand to record your guitar or bass, provided you have the right tools. Since the iPad doesn't have an audio input, you need an audio interface designed for use with an iPad or iPhone (4.25). Apogee Digital and IK Multimedia make some of the more popular options, and many other companies have similar offerings. Most are plug-and-play, meaning all you have to do is plug the interface into your iPhone or iPad and you're ready to start jamming.

4.25 Apogee Jam

For guitarists, a great recording option is GarageBand's virtual guitar amp collection (4.26). GarageBand comes with eight different amps, all emulations of classic guitar rigs from the likes of Vox, Fender, Marshall, and Orange. With this kind of variety on offer, it's possible to get a huge range of sounds even if you only have one guitar. GarageBand includes clean tones, crunchy and distorted options, and even heavily processed sounds.

4.26 Virtual guitar amps

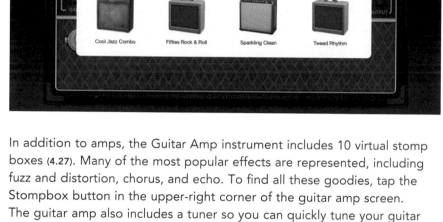

In addition to amps, the Guitar Amp instrument includes 10 virtual stomp boxes (4.27). Many of the most popular effects are represented, including fuzz and distortion, chorus, and echo. To find all these goodies, tap the Stompbox button in the upper-right corner of the guitar amp screen. The guitar amp also includes a tuner so you can quickly tune your guitar between takes (4.28).

If you're a bass player, your options are more limited. Unlike the Mac version of GarageBand, the iOS version doesn't include any bass amps. But that doesn't mean you can't record your bass. You still have the option of choosing the Audio Recorder, which is a basic audio track with no bells and whistles.

The process is simple. Connect your bass as you would an electric guitar, and instead of choosing the Guitar Amp instrument, select Audio Recorder. Tap the Record button and groove!

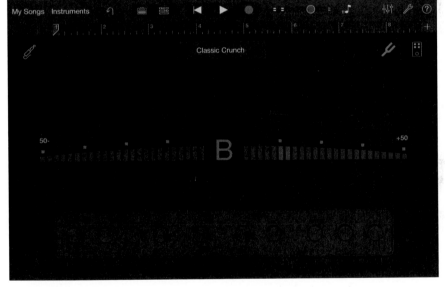

▶ **TIP** Don't be disappointed about the lack of bass amps in the iOS version of GarageBand. Thousands of famous recordings feature bass recorded directly into the recording console instead of through an amp, and many bass players prefer the cleaner, punchier sound that results from recording this way.

Share the Song with iMovie

When it's time to get your musical masterpiece out of GarageBand and into iMovie, you can share the song directly between apps.

Sharing a song with iMovie is a relatively simple process.

1. Open the My Songs browser.

2. Tap Select, and tap the song you want to open in iMovie (4.29).

4.29 Yes, those icons are askew. They shake when you're in the selection mode.

3. Tap the Share button.

4. Tap the Open In button.

5. Enter the optional artist, composer, and album info, and select an appropriate audio quality (4.30).

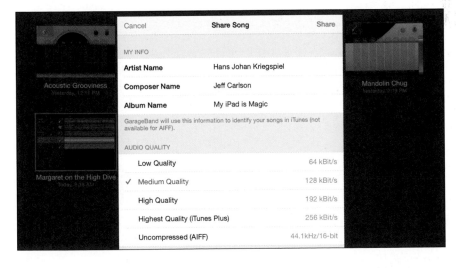

4.30 Adding info and choosing audio quality

6. Tap Share. GarageBand exports the song.

7. When prompted, select Open in iMovie (4.31).

8. In iMovie, select a project or create a new movie (4.32). The song is dropped onto the audio track (4.33).

4.31 Open in iMovie.

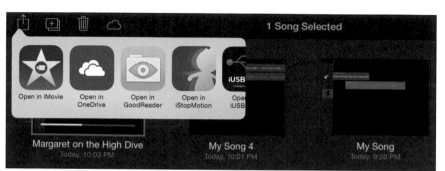

4.32 Choose an iMovie project.

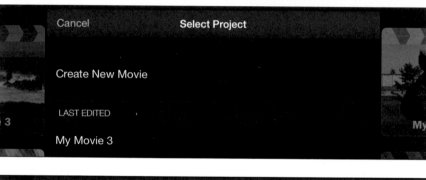

4.33 Song added in iMovie

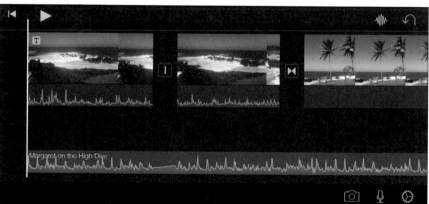

► **TIP** Higher quality settings result in larger audio files, and often you'll need to balance quality and size. For final audio, select High Quality and above. If your song isn't finished and you just need to check timing and feel, one of the lower quality settings will work fine.

► **TIP** Your soundtrack doesn't need to be completely finished to add it to your video. You'll often want to import a rough version into iMovie to make sure everything lines up or that the music feels right. In these cases, follow the same instructions for sharing with iMovie, but know that you may need to open the song again in GarageBand, make changes, and then re-share (possibly even multiple times) in order to finalize your soundtrack.

Going Further with GarageBand

Since this book is about video and not music, it isn't possible to cover all the nuances of GarageBand here. There are, however, great resources available, even within the program itself. The manual is always only a few taps away. On the iPad, tap the Info button, and then tap "Learn more about the control bar." You can access the complete manual by tapping the Table of Contents icon in the upper left, or search the manual by tapping the Search button. On the iPhone, tap the Settings button and scroll to the bottom of the Song settings to open GarageBand Help.

The iOS version of GarageBand has a lot of great features, but many more editing and mixing options are available on the Mac version. To share a GarageBand for iOS project with GarageBand for Mac, you have two options: iCloud and iTunes.

Share via iCloud

To share a project via iCloud, navigate to the My Songs window and tap Select. Choose the song, tap the iCloud button, and choose Upload Song to iCloud **(4.34, on the next page)**. The song becomes available on all devices that use your iCloud account.

4.34 iCloud upload

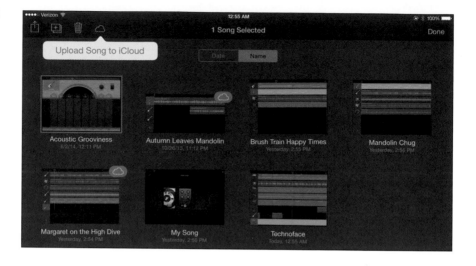

Share via iTunes

In this scenario, iTunes acts as a go-between to transfer the project file from the iPhone or iPad to GarageBand on the Mac.

1. Open the My Songs window and select the project.

2. This time, tap the Share icon and select iTunes, then choose the GarageBand option to save the multitrack GarageBand project (4.35).

    The song's file is saved in a special storage area of the device reserved for GarageBand that iTunes can access.

3. Connect your iOS device to your computer.

4. On your Mac, select the device in iTunes and click the Apps tab.

5. Scroll down to the File Sharing section and click the GarageBand icon.

6. Select the project and drag it to your desktop; or, click the Save To button and choose a location (4.36).

    You may see a message saying that GarageBand has to download additional content to your Mac for compatibility. This shouldn't take long, and only has to happen the first time you open GarageBand for iOS projects on your Mac.

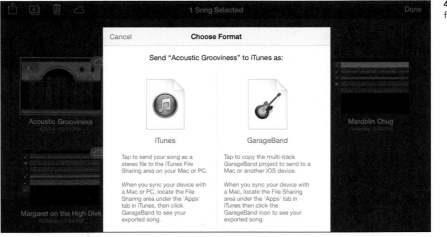

4.35 Saving the file for iTunes

4.36 The project in iTunes

CHAPTER 5

Create Stop-Motion and Time-Lapse Movies

Most of this book is about live-action movies, where you record events in real time and edit them together. But that's just one type of video you can create. Since a movie is just a series of single frames played sequentially, you can string together individual shots to make stop-motion animations. The *Wallace and Grommet* shorts (or the *Shaun the Sheep* spinoff TV series) and movies such as *Fantastic Mr. Fox* and *The Nightmare Before Christmas* (to name some favorites) are all examples of stop-motion animation.

A related type of video is the time-lapse movie. In this style, the camera is mostly stationary and captures photos on a preset schedule. You can compress hours of real time into a couple of minutes

Stop-Motion Movies

Rather than point the camera and record whatever action occurs, stop-motion animation involves you moving elements within a scene in small increments. When the footage is played back at normal speed, the elements appear to move and interact. It requires a lot of patience to do well, but the reward is being able to construct almost anything your imagination can come up with.

On iOS, my favorite tool for creating stop-motion animations is Boinx's iStopMotion for iPad, which I'll use to demonstrate how to film and share a movie. Similar apps exist, and I encourage you to give them a try. The downside to iStopMotion is that it doesn't run on the iPhone (although you can control it from the iPad using the free iStopCamera app). If the iPhone is your only camera, consider Stop Motion Studio, which works similarly to iStopMotion.

Build the Set

Time to strap on your carpenter's toolbelt and get to work, even before you capture a single frame of the movie. Since you'll be shooting over a long period of time, it's important to record in an area that has consistent light, room for you to work, and a place where you can set the camera without moving it.

Choose and lock down your camera

If you own just one iOS device, your choice is made. But if you own more than one device, I recommend using the one that can be easily mounted and left in place. Unless you know your movie will be short and captured in one session, you probably don't want to use the iPhone you carry with you all the time. It will be harder to match the previous shot if you need to re-align the iPhone (although it's not impossible, thanks to the "onion skin" feature I'll describe later in this chapter).

Stop-motion animation is a situation where you definitely want to lock the iPhone, iPad, or iPod touch into a stable position (5.1). (See Chapter 1 for suggestions for tripods and mounts.) Or, if you want the camera to be mobile, employ a slider or other device that lets you move the camera incrementally.

▶ **TIP** To help you line up your composition, turn on the app's grid lines. Tap the Clip Settings button (the gear icon) and enable the Grid Lines option.

Lighting

Yes, you need light on your stop-motion set, but the important consideration is that you need *consistent* light. Since you're trying to simulate real time (or something close to it), the gradual shift of daylight that is normal to us becomes exaggerated in the video.

If possible, record in an area that has no windows, or block out natural light (or make your movie only at night). Doing so also avoids color shifts that can occur due to moving cloud cover and time of day.

The lights you use can be anything from always-on studio lights to inexpensive work lights bought at the hardware store.

Accessibility

Make sure you can access the elements of the scene easily without disturbing them or bumping the camera. That can be as simple as leaving enough room to work or as complex as building a trap door (which is what the special effects technicians did to film the AT-AT walkers in *The Empire Strikes Back*).

Lock the Capture Settings

Now that you've set up a movie set, it's time to start making the movie. The first step is to lock the focus, exposure, and white balance settings to ensure those aspects are consistent between frames.

1. Open iStopMotion and create a new project (which the app calls a clip).

2. Tap once on the middle of the screen to reveal the toolbar.

3. Tap the Sources button (the video camera icon) (5.2).

4. Tap the Settings button. The Focus settings are selected.

5. Tap the area of the scene you want to keep in focus.

6. To adjust the exposure of the scene, tap the Exposure button and drag the reticule to identify a tone on which to base how bright or dark the scene is (5.3).

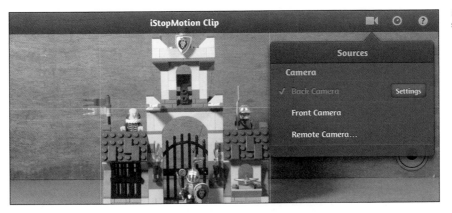

Initially the Exposure is set to Continuous, which adjusts the exposure if the light changes or you reposition the iOS device. To lock the level you set, tap the Continuous button so it reads Fixed instead.

7. To set the scene's color temperature, tap the White Balance button.

   By default, the control automatically adjusts to changes in the scene (the Unlocked setting). White Balance doesn't offer a specific control, so do this: Position a sheet of white paper in the middle of the scene and wait for the app to compensate the balance; then, tap the Unlocked button so it reads Locked.

8. Tap Done to apply the settings.

5.3 Setting exposure

> ► **NOTE** Remember, you can also disregard all of this advice and make a great stop-motion movie without a set, consistent lighting, or a tripod. In fact, I've learned firsthand that an iPad and some readily available objects are perfect distractions for kids on long flights or train rides (5.4).

5.4 A sequence from my daughter's stop-motion epic *Elsa Eats a Cracker on the Plane*

Choose a Frame Rate

You remember from earlier that the Camera app shoots at 30 frames per second (fps), and other apps can capture at 24 or 25 fps, which is the normal rate for film projection. So what frame rate is used for stop-motion animation? iStopMotion defaults to 12 fps, but you can choose any amount you like. What's important to keep in mind is that the higher the frame rate, the more total frames you need to complete the clip (so it will take longer to shoot). Also, you need to move objects in smaller, finer increments or risk making it look like everything has been sped up.

To choose a frame rate, tap the Clip Settings button and next to Speed (frames/sec.) tap the − or + button (5.5).

Record the Movie

With the set and the "talent" in place, it's time to start the painstakingly slow process of capturing frames. Remember to be patient and move objects in small increments—or move them in larger increments if they need to appear to move quickly.

1. Tap the Capture button to record a frame. It appears in the timeline at the bottom of the screen.

   ▶ **TIP** Touch and hold the Capture button to insert a black or white frame.

2. Move an object in your scene to the next position. Notice that the new placement appears as a partially transparent overlay (5.6). This "onion skin" effect enables you to compare the last recorded frame with the new movement.

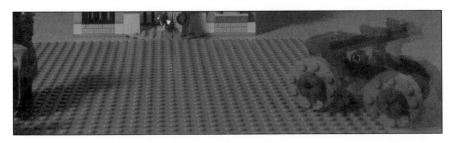

5.6 Onion skin effect

3. Tap the Capture button to capture the next frame.

4. Repeat steps 1–3 as needed hundreds or thousands of times to make the movie (5.7).

At any point, tap the Play button at left to play the video at the speed you've set in the Clip settings. It's often helpful to review the clip at a slower pace: enable the Play Half Speed option in the Clip settings. To view any frame, scroll left or right or tap a frame directly.

▶ **TIP** Scroll the timeline with two fingers to jump to the beginning or end of the clip.

▶ **TIP** If, for some reason, playback is skipping or otherwise isn't working correctly, the video may need to be re-rendered. Touch and hold the Play button for a few seconds to let iStopMotion create a new preview version.

5.7 Intrigue in 58 frames (so far)

Edit as You Capture

You don't need to trim clips by slicing the ends the way you do in iMovie, since each frame is its own image. If you mess up a frame, for example, it's easy to re-capture it.

Tap the Actions button (the wrench icon) on the current frame to reveal the following options (5.8).

- **Delete Frame(s):** The first two options let you delete the current frame or all frames in the clip.

- **Duplicate Frame:** Choose this option to add time without adding any motion to the video. Duplicating can be helpful when you want to add a pause, or maybe insert dialogue without moving objects.

- **Reverse Order of Frames:** Pretend you're Superman flying clockwise around the earth at impossible speeds.

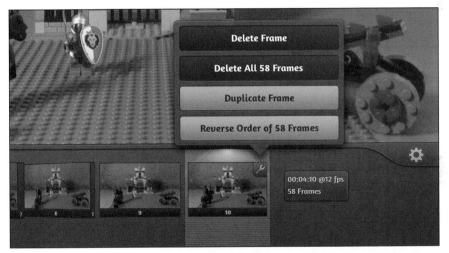

5.8 Frame options

> ▶ **TIP** A quicker way to delete a single clip is to drag it up to the viewer.

> ▶ **TIP** You can change the focus point at any time while you're recording (such as when you have objects in the foreground and background). If you don't want an abrupt focus shift across two frames, tap intervening areas between objects for a few frames to create a transition.

Add Audio

iStopMotion supports adding audio to the clip, although the feature is limited to just one piece of audio. That can be a song from your iTunes library, audio from SoundCloud or Dropbox, or audio you record directly in the app.

In nearly all animated movies, dialogue is recorded before the frames are drawn or captured, so the video can be tailored to fit the audio. If you're creating a scripted scene, record the dialogue first and then bring it into iStopMotion.

If you're looking to layer sound effects as well, it's better to bring the clip into iMovie and add them there. iStopMotion isn't designed to build a full movie—which is why each project is referred to as a "clip."

Import to Audio Library

To add audio, do the following:

1. Tap the Audio button above the timeline and choose Audio Library.

2. Choose a source: Music Library, SoundCloud, or Dropbox.

3. Navigate to the audio file you want and tap it. The file is copied to iStopMotion's library (5.9). Tap the play button at right to preview the audio, or tap the name of the audio file to add it to the clip.

▶   **NOTE** Songs you record in GarageBand—or any app that supports the Open In feature—can also be imported. When you share the piece, tap the Open In button and choose iStopMotion. The file is added to the Audio Library.

 5.9 Audio Library

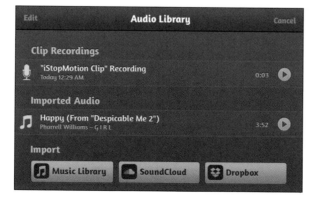

Record audio

Flex your vocal talents (or sound-effects abilities) by recording something on the spot.

1. Tap the Audio button above the timeline and choose Record.

2. When you're ready, tap the Record button (5.10). The app gives you a countdown from 3 and starts recording.

3. Tap Stop to end recording.

4. To preview the recording, tap the Play button. If the audio sounds good, tap the Use button. Or, tap Record Again to give it another shot. The audio appears below the video in blue.

▶ **NOTE** The Record feature will store as much audio as you give it, regardless of the length of your clip. To hold it back, tap the sound-wave button to the right of the Record button and enable the option "Limit audio recording to current length of clip."

5.10 Preparing to record

Position audio

Audio is automatically placed at the start of the first frame, but you can offset its position so the sound begins where you want.

1. Tap the Actions button (the wrench icon) for the audio track to view audio options.

2. Tap the – or + button next to Offset to advance or back up full frames (5.11). Use the waveforms as a guide to line up the start of the audio with the frame you want. You can also drag the track to position the audio in partial-frame increments.

3. Optionally set a Fade In and Fade Out duration.

4. Tap outside the popover to dismiss it and apply the changes.

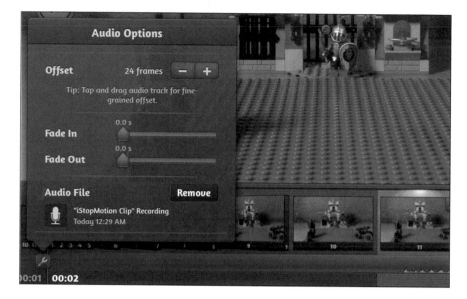

5.11 Audio options

Remove the audio

To delete the audio track, do one of the following:

- Tap the Audio button above the timeline and choose Remove Audio (it's the only option if an audio track is present).

- Tap the Actions button on the audio track and then tap Remove in the Audio Options popover.

Share the Animation

When you're finished with the clip, you can share it in several ways (Dropbox, email, YouTube, WebDAV server, even as animated GIFs), but the easiest is saving it to the Camera Roll (and subsequently importing into iMovie). But first, it's time to name your work something other than "iStopMotion Clip 12."

1. Tap the screen to reveal the toolbar, and then tap Gallery.

2. Tap the title of your clip and give it a new name.

3. Tap Done.

To share the clip, tap the Share button at the bottom of the screen to bring up the sharing options, and then choose an outlet (5.12). (Chapter 6 includes more detailed information about sharing videos, such as the steps to share to the Camera Roll and YouTube.)

5.12 Sharing options

Time-Lapse Movies

Both stop-motion and time-lapse movies capture their subjects one frame at a time, but the latter involves much less work. A time-lapse recording captures each frame on a schedule, such as every minute, such that when it's played back, time is compressed. iStopMotion for iPad features a basic time-lapse feature that captures a frame at a specific interval. On the iPhone, I like the app Lapse It to accomplish the same feat.

To start iStopMotion recording a time-lapse clip, do the following:

1. Open iStopMotion and create a new clip, just as you did at the beginning of this chapter.

2. Tap once on the screen to view the toolbar.

3. Lock the focus, exposure, and white balance if you wish (as described earlier).

4. Tap the Time Lapse button to view the time-lapse options.

5. Change the mode from Single to Time Lapse.

6. Set an interval—the time between captures (5.13). Tap outside the popover to dismiss it.

7. Tap the Capture button to begin shooting. The button turns into a countdown timer indicating the next shot.

8. When you're done recording, tap the Capture button again to stop.

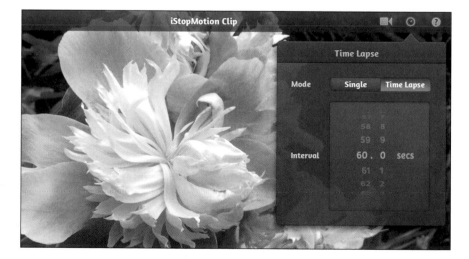

5.13 Time Lapse settings

CHAPTER 6

Share Videos

To paraphrase a popular Internet meme, share your movie or it didn't happen.

The videos you shoot and edit are great for saving a lasting archive of memories, much like the old 8mm film reels your parents (or grandparents) used to pull out once a year. But with several instantly gratifying Internet sharing services just a tap away, there's no need to hold back. Upload movies to your Facebook account or the You-Tube and Vimeo video sharing sites, or even share newsworthy videos to CNN iReport. And if you and your family are heavily invested in Apple's iCloud ecosystem, you can share videos to iCloud Photo Streams or iMovie Theater, where you can play them on an Apple TV or any other iOS device connected to your iCloud account.

You can also share videos from your iOS device to the big screen by wirelessly broadcasting them to an Apple TV using Apple's AirPlay feature. This is especially handy when you want to show off your iMovie projects while visiting a friend's or relative's home or while presenting at a conference.

Finally, I'll take a look at a couple of storytelling apps on the iPad that enable you to quickly pull together photos, graphics, videos, and voiceover to create video stories that you can share on the Web.

Save to the Camera Roll

Your first sharing option is actually a saving action. Saving a final version of the movie to the Camera Roll makes the video available not only in the Photos app, but also from other apps that can access the device's default media library. I'm describing how to do it from iMovie, but the process is similar in any app that offers to save video.

1. In iMovie, tap the Projects button and select the project to share.

2. Tap the Share button on the individual project view (6.1).

3. Tap the Save Video button on the Share popover.

4. In the dialog that appears, choose a resolution to export:
   Medium - 360p, Large - 540p, HD - 720p, or HD - 1080p.
   iMovie creates the finished movie and saves it to the Camera Roll.

5. To view the movie there, open the Photos app, locate the movie at the bottom of the library, and tap the Play button.

6.1 The individual project view (left) and share sheet with sharing options (right)

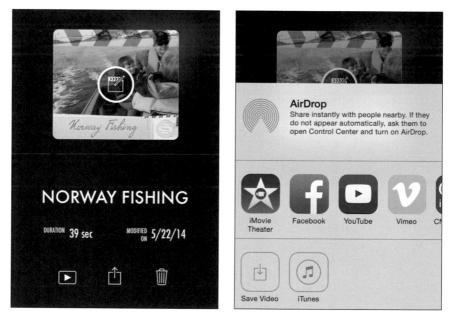

▶ **TIP** The Albums view in the Photos app includes an album called Videos, which automatically includes any videos present in the library.

Send to an iCloud Shared Photo Stream

Apple's iCloud service provides a couple of ways to share videos with others. iMovie Theater, which I talk about shortly, is great for viewing completed movies within iMovie and on an Apple TV. But I also like iCloud Shared Photo Stream, which lets me create a shared album that can be viewed by anyone with an iCloud account. For example, I created a Shared Photo Stream to collect photos and videos of my daughter; when I add an item to it, everyone in my family with an iPhone or iPad is notified that something new is available. I don't have to send an email (and risk forgetting to include someone) or point people to a specific Web address. The video or photo just appears.

1. In the Photos app, tap to select a movie.

2. Tap the Share button.

3. On the sharing screen that appears, tap the iCloud button.

4. Add an optional comment about the video, and tap the Stream button to select a shared stream (6.2). You can also create a new stream.

5. Tap Post to share the video.

6.2 Sending to an iCloud Shared Photo Stream

Share to Internet Services

You can share both completed iMovie projects (from the Projects view) and individual clips (from the Video view) to several Internet sharing sites built into the share sheet, including Facebook, YouTube, Vimeo, and CNN iReport, as well as to Apple's own iMovie Theater. The posting process is straightforward and fairly similar for each of the four sharing services, differing largely in what privacy levels are available from the service.

Share to Facebook, YouTube, Vimeo, or CNN iReport

1. Go to the Projects screen and then tap the project you want to share.

2. Tap the Share button (6.3).

6.3 Sharing a project

▶ **TIP** I'm assuming you want to share your edited movie, but you can also share individual clips from the Video screen by using the same steps. Some options, such as simultaneously adding a movie to iMovie Theater while sharing to an online service, are not available when sharing single clips.

3. Tap the button of your desired sharing service. If you haven't signed in to the service, enter your credentials and tap OK when asked to grant iMovie access to that account.

4. When sharing an edited iMovie project, you'll see the Add to Theater option at the top (6.4). Turn the option on to upload this project to iMovie Theater at the same time it's shared to the selected service.

6.4 Uploading a video to YouTube

5. Tap the title field to edit it. (Projects retain the name given to the project.) Tap the description field below to add more about your movie.

6. For YouTube uploads, tap the category pop-up and scroll to the one that best fits your video.

7. For YouTube and Vimeo uploads, add identifying keywords, separated by commas, to the Tags field.

8. Tap one of the available resolutions under Size. In addition to the recommended default of 540p, you can go larger (720p or 1080p, depending on your movie's resolution) or smaller (360p).

9. Each sharing service has a different scheme for addressing privacy (and even different naming conventions for the privacy field).

- **Facebook:** Under Viewable By, choose Only Me (default), Only Friends, Friends of Friends, or Everyone.

- **YouTube:** Under Privacy, choose Private (default, seen only by you and the users you select via Google+), Unlisted (seen only by those with the link to the video), or Public.

- **Vimeo:** Under Viewable By, choose Nobody Else (default), My Contacts, or Anyone.

- **CNN iReport:** No privacy controls are included.

10. For YouTube uploads, tap the Location field; a pop-up asks if you'd like to get the location from the project. If you've added location information to your project, tapping Yes automatically fills in the locale that you set up (even if it's custom text). If you tap Yes and you haven't added a location to your project (or you tap No), type a location or leave the field blank.

11. Tap Share in the upper-right corner to begin uploading to the service (and to iMovie Theater, if you enabled the Add to Theater option). The movie is exported and then uploaded to the service.

▶ **TIP** It might seem counterintuitive to choose as a default to hide videos under a shroud of privacy when you share them. But doing so can give you additional time to review the video on the service's Web site and make any other modifications to the description, title, keywords, or thumbnail before opening the video to a wider audience. The trick is remembering that you marked it private. Facebook does a good job of reminding you that an uploaded video is marked to be viewed only by you by giving it a chevron border when you view it in your timeline (6.5).

▶ **TIP** If you share a project to multiple services and keep the Add to Theater option on for each upload, you'll end up with multiple videos of the same project in iMovie Theater.

When the upload has been published to a sharing service, you're given three options: Visit, Tell a Friend, and Close (6.6).

- Tap Visit to open the video's post on the sharing service's Web site via Safari. You'll need to be signed in with your credentials in order to see videos uploaded with the most restrictive privacy.

Agen Schmitz
2 minutes ago via iMovie 🔒 **Only Me**

Norway Fishing
Fishing with Ottar and the boys.

Fishing, The Norwegian Way

0:39

Like · Comment · Promote · Share

6.5 A video marked as Only Me on the Facebook Web site offers visual cues to its privacy sandbox.

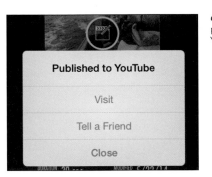

6.6 Options after publishing a video to YouTube

- Tap Tell a Friend to open another share sheet with options to share the link via Messages text, Twitter tweet, Facebook post, or email message. Or, tap the Copy button to copy a link to the post to the Clipboard.

- Tap Close to dismiss the dialog.

► **TIP** If you previously shared a project or clip to a sharing service, tapping the Share button displays the above three options as well as Publish Again (in case you want to upload the video to a new post).

► **NOTE** If you have Google two-step authentication turned on, you'll need to generate an application-specific password to access your account in the YouTube app. (If you sign in to the YouTube Web site in Safari, you'll be prompted to enter a special code sent to you via text message or email.) To generate this password, sign in to your Google account, go to the Security page (www.google.com/settings/security), and click the Settings link for app passwords. In the Name field, type a name for this password (such as "YouTube for iPhone"), then click the Generate Password button. Enter the 16-character password that's generated (without spaces) into the Password field of the Sign in to YouTube pop-up, and then tap Sign In.

Share via Messages or Mail

If you have contacts with whom you'd like to share a video directly, you can share iMovie projects and video clips via text message or email (6.7). Note, however, that you won't be sending a link to view the shared video, but a video file that might take time and bandwidth both to upload from your iOS device and for your recipient to download.

Share via Messages

1. Tap Projects and then tap the project you want to share (the view shifts to the invidual project view). Or, tap Video and then tap a desired clip to select it to play.

2. Tap the Share button on the individual project view or on the Video view (upper-right corner in landscape orientation, lower-right in portrait).

3. Tap the Message button to bring up a New Message page.

4. In the To field, type a contact's name, enter the phone number or email address, or tap the plus icon and select a contact. Repeat as needed for additional recipients.

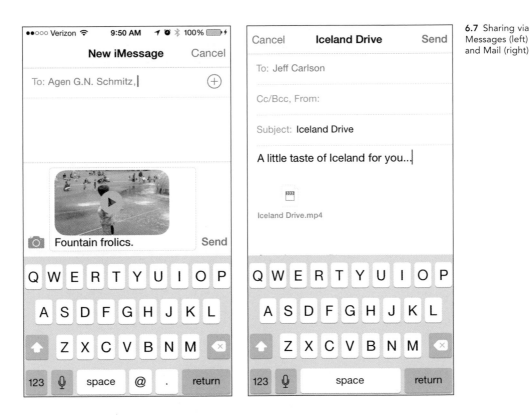

5. Revise the prefilled "Check out my movie!" text in the message bubble if you want, then tap Send.

Share via Mail

1. Go to the Projects screen and tap the project you want to share. Or, tap Video and then tap a desired clip to select it to play.

2. Tap the Share button on the individual project view or on the Video view (upper-right corner in landscape orientation, lower-right in portrait).

3. Tap the Mail button to bring up a new email message.

4. Tap the To field and type a contact's name or email address, or tap the plus icon and select a contact. Repeat as needed for additional recipients in the To, CC, or BCC field.

5. Modify the pre-filled subject line to suit your tastes. It's pre-filled with either the name of the iMovie project or, if sharing a clip from the Video screen, a generically dated video name (such as "Video from May 25, 2014").

6. Tap the body of the email and type a message to go along with your video.

7. Tap Send, or tap Cancel to either save a draft of this email for later or delete the draft completely.

▶ **NOTE** When sharing via Messages or Mail, videos are exported in different resolutions depending on your connectivity when the export process starts. If you're connected to LTE or Wi-Fi, the video will be exported and sent in 640 x 360 resolution, which produces a larger file size (but smaller than sending in either 720p or 1080p HD resolution). If you only have a 3G connection, the video will be exported at a resolution of 352 x 200 pixels.

Share to iMovie Theater

iMovie Theater is essentially a closed service that enables you to upload projects to Apple's iCloud service so you can view videos on Apple TVs and other iOS devices connected to your account. You can also upload any clip from your video library to iMovie Theater without having to first create a project, and you can share projects and clips from iMovie Theater to other sharing services.

Export a Project to iMovie Theater

1. Tap Projects and then tap the project you want to share.

2. Tap the Share button on the individual project view.

3. Tap the iMovie Theater button on the share sheet to begin the export process.

Once exporting is complete, iMovie shifts to Theater view, where you'll find a thumbnail for your movie with the same name you gave your iMovie project (6.8). Tapping the thumbnail opens a detail screen with play, share, and trash buttons (6.9).

▶ **TIP** The movie you just exported to iMovie Theater is essentially an alias of your locally saved movie project. Tap the Edit icon to return to the movie's editing view under Projects.

6.8 iMovie Theater

6.9 The movie's detail screen

► **TIP** Movies uploaded to iMovie Theater from iMovie on a Mac or other iOS devices connected to your iCloud account appear in Theater with a cloud icon in the upper-right corner of the title block to denote that it streams from iCloud. To save a local copy to your iOS device, tap the cloud icon with the down-pointing arrow.

► **TIP** To minimize the bandwidth of videos streaming from iCloud, toggle the HD On button to HD Off so your device streams a lower-resolution (and therefore smaller) version of the video (6.10).

6.10 Toggle between HD On and HD Off to save streaming bandwidth.

Export a Clip to iMovie Theater

1. Tap Video, and then tap a video clip to select it.

2. Tap the Share button.

3. Tap the iMovie Theater button.

4. Enter a name in the Share to Theater pop-up, then tap OK to begin the export process.

As with a project, the video clip gets exported and uploaded to iMovie Theater and appears in the Theater view. Tap a movie to open a play window, where you can tap the play button and start to watch the video.

Share from iMovie Theater

You can share a video uploaded to iMovie Theater to Facebook, YouTube, Vimeo, and CNN iReport, just like you can a project or a clip. However, you'll find a share button only on videos in iMovie Theater that have been saved locally to your device. To share an iMovie Theater video to the Internet, do the following:

1. Tap Theater, and then tap a video to select it.

2. If an iCloud icon appears in the title block, tap the iCloud download icon to download a local copy (6.11). A circular progress icon appears below the video's title. You can tap the X icon that appears to cancel the download.

3. Once the download has finished, the iCloud download icon disappears, and the inactive Share button is replaced by an active icon. Tap that to select your sharing venue, or tap the Save button to save the video to your Camera Roll in Photos.

6.11 Video stored on iCloud

Download from iCloud

Delete from iMovie Theater

To save storage space on your device, try to keep most of your iMovie Theater videos stored in the cloud. To delete a video saved to your iOS device's storage, tap the trash icon and choose one of the following:

- **Remove from device** to delete the local copy.

- **Remove from iCloud** to keep the local copy but delete the iMovie Theater version in the cloud.

- **Delete Everywhere** if you really want to delete with extreme prejudice.

▶ **TIP** Tapping the trash icon in iCloud-based iMovie Theater videos presents only the Delete Everywhere option.

Share via Other Apps

While iMovie provides a number of handy options for sharing videos, the share sheet barely taps into the sharing potential—Wordpress and Tumblr are just two notable omissions. However, you do have the power to upload an iMovie project or iMovie Theater title to a blog or sharing site with the help of the Photos app. Here's one method, using Tumblr as an example, that can be applied to other apps.

Upload a Video to Tumblr

1. In the Projects screen, tap a project; or, in iMovie Theater, tap a movie.

2. Tap the Share button on the movie's detail screen.

3. Tap the Save Video button to add the movie to the device's Camera Roll.

4. Close the iMovie app and open the Tumblr app.

5. Tap the New Post button (the pencil icon) in the Dashboard view. From the choices that pop up, tap the Video button.

6. A new post appears with a popover that opens the Camera Roll. Navigate to the video you want to share, and then tap it to select it.

7. In the Choose Video popover, tap Use (or Cancel to return to the Camera Roll). Tumblr then compresses the video for uploading.

8. A New Post popover appears when processing is completed. Write a caption, add tags, and toggle the Twitter button on to share a tweet. You can also adjust posting options from the settings gear icon, where you can select to post now, add to your queue, save as a draft, or schedule a posting time (6.12).

9. Tap Post at the top of the screen to upload the video to Tumblr, or tap Cancel.

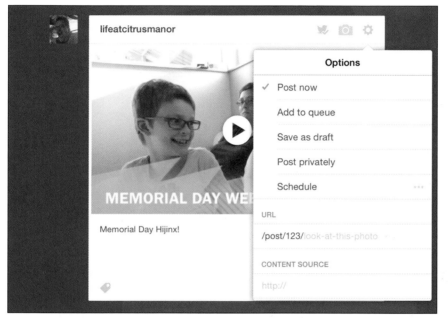

6.12 Tumblr offers several posting options.

Watch on an Apple TV

The easiest way to watch your iMovie projects and video clips on the Apple TV is to export them to iMovie Theater. Additionally, if you've shared videos to YouTube or Vimeo, you can access them via those apps on the Apple TV.

However, if you want to show off videos on an Apple TV that's not connected to your iCloud credentials (or to your accounts for YouTube or Vimeo), you can use Apple's AirPlay Wi-Fi streaming feature to broadcast videos from your iOS device to the screen or a projector connected to an Apple TV.

Watch Using iMovie Theater on Apple TV

Here's how to access the videos you've uploaded to iMovie Theater via an Apple TV:

1. Navigate to the iMovie Theater app on your Apple TV, and select it.

    If you haven't signed in to iCloud on this Apple TV, you'll be asked to sign in. You may be asked if you want to use credentials that have previously been entered elsewhere (such as the iTunes Store). You can also choose to sign in with a different Apple ID. Type your Apple ID (if signing in as a new or different user) and password using the Apple TV remote or the Remote app on your iOS device.

2. The Apple TV connects to your account and then displays the videos that have been exported to iMovie Theater.

3. Navigate to a title using the Apple TV remote or iOS Remote app, and then press either the Play/Pause or Select button on the Apple TV remote or tap your iOS device's screen (if using the Remote app) to begin playing.

Stream iMovie Projects via AirPlay

AirPlay makes it insanely easy to stream videos to an Apple TV. But before you can start streaming videos, make sure that AirPlay is turned on in the Apple TV settings.

Additionally, you may have to jump through a few hoops depending on the AirPlay Security settings that have been configured on the Apple TV to which you want to broadcast. You may have to enter either a password or a four-digit code that appears on the screen. You may also have to enter a code if the Apple TV requires a device to be verified.

Once AirPlay is configured on your Apple TV, here's how to stream an iMovie project from your iPhone or iPad:

1. Go to the Projects screen and then tap the project you want to watch (the view shifts to the individual project view).

2. Tap the AirPlay button in the lower-right corner (6.13).

6.13 AirPlay options

3. Tap the name of the Apple TV in the popover to stream the video to its connected screen.

4. Tap the Play button to start playing the video. Your device's screen displays an AirPlay icon against a dark background while the video plays on the Apple TV.

▶ **NOTE** Projects that haven't previously been exported either to the Camera Roll or to iMovie Theater first need to be prepared for playback via AirPlay. After tapping the AirPlay button, a Preparing Movie for Airplay progress bar appears in the middle of the screen. When the exporting/optimizing process completes, the project starts streaming to the Apple TV. Additionally, if you make edits to a project, the video will have to be prepared again.

5. As the video plays, you can adjust the play position on your iOS device using the scrubber bar at the top of the screen, or tap the Pause

button to stop playback. You can also touch and hold the Reverse and Forward buttons to move through your videos. However, if you simply tap either Reverse or Forward, the video stops playing and returns to the individual project view.

▶ **TIP** When streaming a video to your Apple TV via AirPlay, you can also use the Apple TV remote to control playback.

Now that you're connected via AirPlay, you can select another iMovie project and stream it to the Apple TV. To return to playing video on your iOS device, tap the AirPlay button in the video's play screen and select the name of your device while a video is actively playing. Your video and audio (such as from the Music or Podcasts app) will continue to broadcast to the Apple TV via AirPlay until you turn it off.

You can also deactivate (or activate) AirPlay from Control Center. Place your finger at the bottom of the screen and swipe up to reveal Control Center, then tap the AirPlay button and select a device from the popover.

▶ **TIP** Selecting AirPlay through Control Center also provides a Mirroring option, which enables you to stream exactly what you see and hear on your iOS device. This is a handy option for demonstrating iMovie techniques to a larger audience through the Apple TV, but isn't required for simply playing videos **(6.14)**.

6.14 Tap the AirPlay button in Control Center, where you can select the Mirroring option.

> ▶ **TIP** AirPlay isn't just for streaming video to an Apple TV. You can also stream just the audio from video playback on your device to an Airport Express Wi-Fi base station connected to speakers (6.15). When you tap the AirPlay button on a video (or select it from Control Center), look for an available Airport Express option (denoted by a speaker icon) and select it. Now, your movie will play on your device's screen, but audio will be heard on the connected speakers (which can be handy for showing off video to more than one person).

6.15 Select an Airport Express to stream only audio via AirPlay.

Stream iMovie Theater Titles via AirPlay

Streaming an iMovie Theater title is similar to streaming projects. The only difference is that you can stream video from titles stored in the cloud, essentially using your iOS device as a conduit between iCloud and the Apple TV. In iMovie under the Theater view, tap an iMovie Theater title (with or without a cloud icon) and follow the directions in the previous section for streaming an iMovie project.

> ▶ **TIP** If you have a slow Internet connection, you can turn the HD resolution off to quicken the pace of downloading from iCloud. The video might not look as pristine in its low-pixel form, but you won't have to worry about stoppages due to buffering.

Stream Video Clips via AirPlay

In order to stream content from iMovie using AirPlay, the video must be a project or already exported and uploaded to iMovie Theater. Clips in the Video view cannot be streamed unless they're first made into a project or an iMovie Theater title. However, you can stream individual video clips from the Photos app.

1. Open the Photos app, tap Albums at the bottom of the screen, and then tap the Videos album. This is where all your available video clips are stored.

2. Tap a video to open its play page.

3. Tap the Share button. On the iPad (or in portrait mode on an iPhone or iPod touch), the share sheet appears at the bottom of the screen as you would expect. Additionally, a thumbnail of the video appears at the top of the screen with a circular blue checkmark. You can ignore the checkmark for this exercise, as it's only for selecting multiple videos to share using one of the main sharing options.

   If you're in landscape mode on an iPhone or iPod touch, a larger thumbnail of your selected video appears with the checkmark. Tap Next in the upper-right corner to get to the share sheet (6.16).

4. Tap the AirPlay button, and then select from the available streaming options. After you make your selection, the AirPlay screen disappears and you return to your video's play screen.

6.16 Tapping the Share button in the Photos app on an iPhone or iPod touch in landscape mode

---

5. Tap the play button in the thumbnail to begin playing from the beginning of the video. Or, use the scrubber at the top of the screen to select a starting position, and then tap the blue Play button. The screen on your device turns black with an AirPlay icon to remind you that it's streaming.

6. Tap the screen to bring back the scrubber. You can also tap the Pause button to stop the movie from streaming.

7. When finished streaming your video, tap the Share button and follow the instructions in step 3 for portrait and landscape modes to return to the share sheet.

8. Tap the AirPlay button, and then select your device to turn off AirPlay streaming to the Apple TV (or turn off AirPlay from Control Center).

Send the Project to iTunes

This method of sharing an iMovie project is, quite frankly, a weird workaround, but it has its uses. You can export the project itself—not just a rendered version of the movie—for backing up to your Mac, sending to another iOS device for editing, or importing into iMovie on the Mac. It is, however, a fairly counterintuitive procedure.

Export a Project to iTunes

1. In the Projects screen, select the project you wish to export and tap the Share button.

2. Tap the iTunes button. iMovie packages all the data and resources (including video clips and audio files) and stores them in iMovie's dedicated storage space on the device.

3. Connect the iOS device to your computer; given the potentially large file sizes involved in a video project, you may want to use a USB connection instead of Wi-Fi syncing.

4. On your computer, open iTunes and select the device, which will appear just below the Search field or in the sidebar, if you've opted to show the sidebar (View > Show Sidebar).

5. Click the Apps button at the top of the screen and scroll down to the File Sharing section.

6. Select iMovie in the Apps column.

7. Select the project you exported (6.17) and click the Save To button. Specify a location, such as the Desktop, and click Save To to transfer the file.

▶ **NOTE** In iTunes you can also delete old exported projects by selecting them and pressing the Delete key or choosing Edit > Delete. Doing so removes only the exported file saved for sharing, not the original project in iMovie.

6.17 The exported project in iTunes

Import the Project into iMovie on Another iOS Device

1. Connect the other device to iTunes and select it.

2. Go to the Apps screen, scroll down to the File Sharing section, and select iMovie in the Apps column.

3. Click the Add button and locate the project file you exported in the previous exercise. Or, drag the project from the Finder to the iMovie Documents column. (You don't need to sync the device to copy the file; it's added directly.)

4. Open iMovie on the iPhone or iPad.

5. Although the project now exists on the device, iMovie doesn't yet know about it. Go to the Projects screen and tap the Import button (6.18).

6. In the dialog that appears, tap the name of the project to import it. It appears among your other projects.

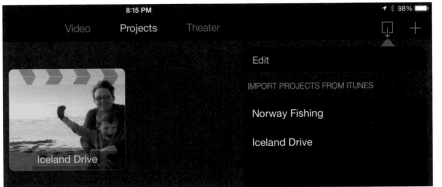

6.18 Importing an iMovie project synced from iTunes

▶ **TIP** This method is also a way to duplicate a project—for example, if you want to save what you've done but try an editing experiment. After sharing to iTunes, tap the Import button to bring a copy back in; it will have a slightly different name.

▶ **TIP** An earlier version of iMovie on the Mac was able to read projects created in iMovie for iOS, which meant you could start editing on your iPhone or iPad, transfer the project through iTunes using the steps described here, and then continue work on the Mac later. Unfortunately, that capability went away with the release of iMovie 10.0 for Mac. I hope a future update restores the feature, as it was awfully handy.

Telling Stories Beyond iMovie

Video is a great way to capture moments, and iMovie is there to help you edit those moments to tell a more complete narrative. But alternatives to iMovie exist that can help you create visually interactive stories—from travelogues and inspiring personal tales to student projects and explainer videos and much more.

Adobe Voice

The free Adobe Voice for iPad app offers an uncomplicated design that combines built-in graphics and animated themes with photos, and you can add your own voice, which you record using the iPad's microphone (hence the name). The simple page-based framework is limited in the choices it offers—from layout options to media that can be added—but this blank-slate approach encourages you to quickly create your narrative without having to fuss over an abundance of feature alternatives.

When you start to create a new story, you're given several options of basic narrative structures (such as Tell What Happened, Promote an Idea, and Teach a Lesson), each of which then provides prompts for telling the story from beginning to end, spread across five to seven pages. Using Follow a Hero's Journey, you're given the following pages: Setup, Call to Adventure, Challenge, Climax, and Resolution. You can follow these prompts, ignore them, or add pages to suit your story.

Once you've selected your narrative path, you can add iconography and photos (but no video) either from your own collections housed on the iPad or in the cloud or from a database of searchable Creative Commons–licensed images and graphics (6.19). You can then tie it together with text and a voiceover before publishing to the Adobe Voice site, from which you can share the video using the usual sharing services and messaging options.

Here's how to get started with Adobe Voice:

1. Open the Adobe Voice app, then tap Create a New Story (visible from the Explore, Projects, and Shared tab views at the top of the screen).

▶ **NOTE** Adobe Voice is limited to displaying in portrait mode.

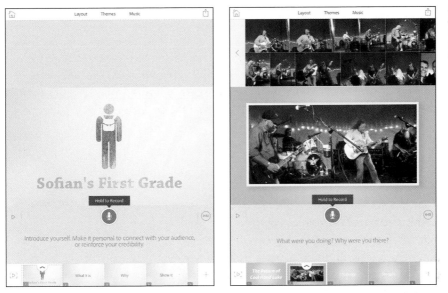

6.19 Adobe Voice enables you add iconography (left) or photos (right) to your story.

2. Type a title for your video, then tap Next. (Or, tap Skip This if you don't have a title in mind yet; you can add a title before you publish.)

3. Choose from one of the story structures: Explain Something, Follow a Hero's Journey, Tell What Happened, Promote an Idea, Share an Invitation, Teach a Lesson, Share a Growth Moment, Make Up My Own, and Show and Tell.

4. Tap Layout at the top of the screen and choose from the limited page design options. For instance, select the Theme + Caption option to create a title for an opening page.

5. Tap the box in the middle of the page and select Icon, Photo, or Text.

6. If you choose Icon, you can search through thousands of royalty-free, Creative Commons–licensed icons (**6.20, on the next page**). Icons fill the height of the box, and their size can't be adjusted.

   With Photo, you can access your own photos from the Camera Roll or ones stored on Dropbox, Adobe Creative Cloud, or Facebook. You can also take a picture with the iPad's camera or find Creative Commons–licensed photos. Pinch to zoom in or out to view more or less detail.

   The Text option enables you to type as much as you wish, and the font size adjusts to the size of the box or caption area.

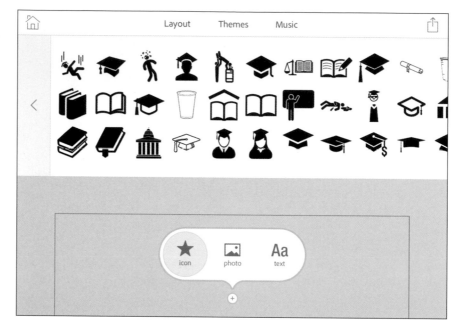

6.20 Tap Icon and search through thousands of royalty-free graphics to add to your story.

7. Tap Themes and navigate through the options to find one that best fits your story. It might seem counterintuitive to choose a theme after starting to build your content, but this way you'll see how Adobe Voice modifies image and text formatting as the app builds a preview to fit each theme.

8. Tap Music to choose from the pre-loaded instrumental pieces, or choose a song stored in the Music app. You can only choose one piece of music to play through a video. Adjust the volume slider to a suitable level.

▶ **TIP** If you want to choose a song that's stored in iCloud (i.e., if you've set the Music app to show all purchases, even those stored in the cloud), you'll be prompted to first download the song file to your iPad.

9. Touch and hold the orange microphone button to record your voice. If you've selected music to play, your voice track plays along with the music. To delete the voice track, tap the circular time button to the right of the microphone and tap Delete Voice Recording.

▶ **TIP** A page will display for a default of 2 seconds, but you can adjust the duration a page displays by tapping the circular time button and adjusting the slider. If you add a voice track, the page will display for only as long as your voice recording lasts.

▶ **TIP** Tap the play button underneath the page you're building to preview just that page. To preview your entire video, tap the play button to the left of the thumbnails.

Repeat this process for subsequent pages. After tapping a page thumbnail to select it, you can tap the arrow at the top of the thumbnail to choose Duplicate Page or Delete from the popover. If you want to add a page, tap the plus sign (+) button at the right.

When you're finished creating and editing your video, tap the Share button in the upper-right corner to view the Upload & Share popover (6.21). You can choose to make the video public (which permits it to be potentially featured in the Adobe Voice gallery) or private (shown only to those with a link to the video). Tap to select a sharing service, to select a messaging service, or to copy the link, then tap the Upload button. You can also tap End Credits to add any additional details (any Creative Commons–licensed media will be credited automatically).

6.21 The Adobe Voice Upload & Share popover

Once the video is uploaded to the Adobe Voice site (voice.adobe.com), you're prompted to write your post, tweet, or message (or have the link copied to the Clipboard).

The video also appears in the Shared view (tap the Home button to return to the Explore, Projects, and Shared tabs), where you can share the link to the same destinations or delete it, or tap the title card of your project to open the Web page in Safari (6.22).

6.22 Share to additional venues by selecting your story from the Shared view.

Upload & Share

The Return of Cool Hand Luke

Cool Hand Luke: The Oles '89 25th Reunion

● Public   Your video can be featured in our gallery

   Private   Only people with the link can view your video

f Share on Facebook   🐦 Share on Twitter

✉ Share by Email   💬 Share by Message

🛍 Copy Link

You'll compose your Facebook post after your video is uploaded   Edit Credits >

Cancel   Upload

Storehouse

An alternative to Adobe Voice is Storehouse.

One disappointment with Adobe Voice is its inability to embed videos you've just edited in iMovie. However, the free Storehouse for iPad app does support adding video clips along with photos and text (6.23). Where Adobe Voice uses a page-based structure, Storehouse gives you a single, scrollable blank canvas that can be as large as you want and filled out with text boxes, photos, and embedded videos. You can add media from the Photos app on your device or from Dropbox, Flickr, and Instagram.

▶ **NOTE** Storehouse limits you to a maximum of 50 photos to a story, and embedded videos can be no longer than 30 seconds. If you try to embed a longer video, you'll get an error message—Storehouse won't allow you to select a 30-second clip from that video.

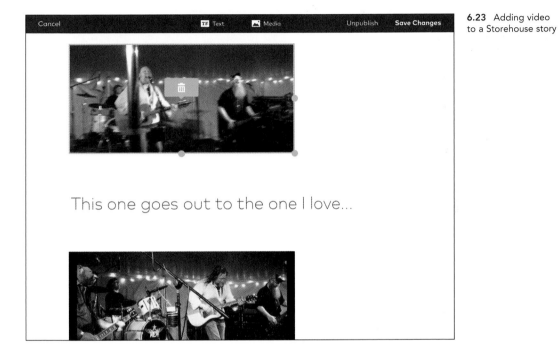

6.23 Adding video to a Storehouse story

When editing them on the iPad or after publishing to the Storehouse Web site, the videos automatically play as you scroll over them (on the Web site, they're muted by default). And, as you might expect, you have options to share your Storehouse creation to Facebook and Twitter as well as via email from the Storehouse app and Web site (with the latter also offering an embed code for adding to a Wordpress or Tumblr blog).

ZeroShake for iPad (Sarapan)

http://www.zeroshake.com/
https://itunes.apple.com/us/app/zeroshake-for-ipad/id7296

ZeroShake for iPhone (Sarapan), Free
(with in-app purchases)

http://www.zeroshake.com/
https://itunes.apple.com/us/app/zeroshake/id616054542

Chapter 3: Edit Video

Emulsio (Creaceed), Free (with in-app purcha

http://www.creaceed.com/emulsio/about
https://itunes.apple.com/us/app/emulsio-powerful-vide
id397583851

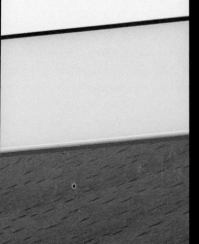

App and Equipment Reference

I knew there would be a lot of apps and equipment mentioned in this book when I started, but I didn't want to pepper every paragraph with an app name, the price, and a lengthy link to the iTunes Store. Instead, this handy reference breaks down all the apps and add-ons mentioned throughout each chapter, organized alphabetically, so you can find and investigate the apps easily. Where possible, I've included links to developers' Web sites, which often feature videos of the apps in action and more detail than what appears at the iTunes Store.

The iTunes Store links are regular Web addresses: Plug them into your favorite Web browser, which will redirect you to the product's page in iTunes. (Note that prices are current as of press time but may change by the time you read this.)

Chapter 1: Video Crash Course

GorillaPod tripod (Joby), various models, $14.95 to $49.95
http://joby.com/gorillapod

Glif iPhone tripod mount (Studio Neat), $30
http://www.studioneat.com/products/glif

iPro Lens System (Schneider Optics), various models, $39.00 to $229.00
http://www.iprolens.com/

iRig Microphone (IK Multimedia), $59.99
http://www.ikmultimedia.com/products/irigmic/

iRig Pre Microphone Interface (IK Multimedia), $39.99
http://www.ikmultimedia.com/products/irigpre/

iStabilizer Dolly (iStabilizer), $49.95
http://www.istabilizer.com/products/istabilizer-dolly

KV Connection
http://www.kvconnection.com/

mCAMLITE case (Action Life Media), $129.95
http://www.actionlifemedia.com/mcamlite

Mobislyder track (Mobislyder), £45.00
http://www.mobislyder.com/

MovieSlate (PureBlend Software), $29.99
http://www.movie-slate.com/
https://itunes.apple.com/us/app/movieslate-clapperboard-shot/id320315888

Olloclip lenses, various models (Olloclip), $49.99 to $99.99
http://www.olloclip.com/

The Padcaster iPad mounts (Padcaster), $99.00 to $149.00

http://thepadcaster.com/

Phocus Accent (Smart Phocus), $39.95

http://smartphocus.com/phocus-accent/

PhotoProX waterproof case (Optrix), $149.95

http://www.optrix.com/store/optrix-photoprox/

smartLav Microphone (Røde), $60.00

http://www.smartlav.com/

VideoMic Pro Microphone (Røde), $229.00

http://www.rodemic.com/microphones/videomicpro

Chapter 2: Capture Video

8mm Vintage Camera (Nexvio), $1.99

http://8mm.mobi/

https://itunes.apple.com/us/app/8mm-vintage-camera/id406541444

8mm for iPad (Nexvio), $1.99

http://8mm.mobi/

https://itunes.apple.com/us/app/8mm-for-ipad/id441875100

FiLMiC Pro (FiLMic), $4.99

http://filmicpro.com/

https://itunes.apple.com/us/app/filmic-pro/id436577167

Final Cut Pro X (Apple), $299.99

http://www.apple.com/final-cut-pro/

https://itunes.apple.com/us/app/final-cut-pro/id424389933?mt=12

GoPro App (Woodman Labs), Free

http://gopro.com/software-app/gopro-app/

https://itunes.apple.com/us/app/gopro-app/id561350520

Horizon (Evil Window Dog), $1.99

http://www.evilwindowdog.com/horizon/

https://itunes.apple.com/us/app/horizon-horizontal-hd-video/id778576249

Instagram (Instagram), Free

http://instagram.com/

https://itunes.apple.com/us/app/instagram/id389801252

Vine (Vine Labs), Free

https://vine.co/

https://itunes.apple.com/us/app/vine/id592447445

Ultrakam (Hassan Uriostegui), $4.99

http://vfxwarrior.com/ultrakam/

https://itunes.apple.com/us/app/ultrakam4k.-upload-4k-quality/id866641004

Ultrakam Pro (Hassan Uriostegui), $6.99

http://vfxwarrior.com/ultrakam/

https://itunes.apple.com/us/app/ultrakam-pro.-professional/id824589326

ZeroShake for iPad (Sarapan), Free (with in-app purchases)

http://www.zeroshake.com/

https://itunes.apple.com/us/app/zeroshake-for-ipad/id729685941

ZeroShake for iPhone (Sarapan), Free (with in-app purchases)

http://www.zeroshake.com/

https://itunes.apple.com/us/app/zeroshake/id616054542

Chapter 3: Edit Video

Emulsio (Creaceed), Free (with in-app purchases)

http://www.creaceed.com/emulsio/about

https://itunes.apple.com/us/app/emulsio-powerful-video-stabilization/id397583851

iMovie for iOS (Apple), $4.99
http://www.apple.com/ios/imovie/
https://itunes.apple.com/us/app/imovie/id377298193

Pinnacle Studio (Corel Inc.), $12.99
http://www.pinnaclesys.com/PublicSite/us/Products/studio/ipad/
https://itunes.apple.com/us/app/pinnacle-studio/id552100086

VideoGrade (Fidel Lainez), $4.99
http://www.flainezapps.com/videograde/
https://itunes.apple.com/us/app/videograde-color-editor-for/id492488712

Chapter 4: Compose a Soundtrack in GarageBand

Apogee Jam guitar input (Apogee)
http://www.apogeedigital.com/products/jam

Audiofile Calc (Audiofile Engineering), Free
http://www.audiofile-engineering.com/triumph/
https://itunes.apple.com/us/app/audiofile-calc/id337547274

GarageBand (Apple), Free (with in-app purchases)
http://www.apple.com/ios/garageband/
https://itunes.apple.com/us/app/garageband/id408709785

Chapter 5: Create Stop-Motion and Time-Lapse Movies

iStopMotion for iPad (Boinx), $9.99
http://boinx.com/istopmotion/ipad/
https://itunes.apple.com/us/app/istopmotion-for-ipad/id484019696

iStopMotion Remote Camera (Boinx), Free

http://boinx.com/istopmotion/ipad/

https://itunes.apple.com/us/app/istopmotion-remote-camera/id484024876

Stop Motion Studio (Cateater, LLC), Free

http://www.cateater.com/#stopmotionstudio

https://itunes.apple.com/us/app/stop-motion-studio/id441651297

Lapse It (Interactive Universe), Free

http://www.lapseit.com/

https://itunes.apple.com/us/app/lapse-it-time-lapse-stop-motion/id539108382

Chapter 6: Share Videos

Adobe Voice for iPad (Adobe Systems, Inc.), Free

http://getvoice.adobe.com/

https://itunes.apple.com/us/app/adobe-voice-show-your-story/id852555131

Storehouse for iPad (Storehouse), Free

https://www.storehouse.co/

https://itunes.apple.com/us/app/storehouse-visual-storytelling/id791297521

Tumblr (Tumblr, Inc.), Free

http://www.tumblr.com/

https://itunes.apple.com/us/app/tumblr/id305343404

Vimeo (Vimeo, LLC), Free

https://www.vimeo.com/

https://itunes.apple.com/us/app/vimeo/id425194759

YouTube (Google, Inc.), Free

https://www.youtube.com/

https://itunes.apple.com/us/app/youtube/id544007664

INDEX

volume
    changing in clips, 85
    changing in loops, 103
    changing in tracks, 106–107
    recorded music, 118

W

waterproof camera cases, 18
waveforms, 85, 86, 88, 118, 140
Web site, companion to book, xiv
WebDAV server, sharing via, 140
white balance, 33, 54, 133
The Wirecutter site, 18
wireless connections, 60

X

XLR-style plug, 11

Y

YouTube, 140, 148–152, 180

Z

ZeroShake app, 40, 52, 178
ZeroShake for iPad, 178
ZeroShake for iPhone, 178
zoom control, 33–35, 69